STANDING GUARD

STANDING GUARD

A YEAR IN OPPOSITION

P. Chidambaram

RUPA

THE
EXPRESS
GROUP

EXPRESS
BOOK
SERIES
TM

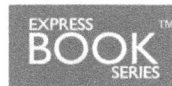

Published by
Rupa Publications India Pvt. Ltd 2016
7/16, Ansari Road, Daryaganj
New Delhi 110002

Sales Centres:

Allahabad Bengaluru Chennai
Hyderabad Jaipur Kathmandu
Kolkata Mumbai

Reprinted from *The Indian* EXPRESS

The views and opinions expressed in this book are the author's own and the
facts are as reported by him which have been verified to the extent possible,
and the publishers are not in any way liable for the same.

ISBN: 978-81-291-3962-7

First impression 2016

10 9 8 7 6 5 4 3 2 1

The moral right of the author has been asserted.

Printed by XXXXXX

CONTENTS

FOREWORD

Y.V. Reddy
former Governor, Reserve Bank of India

The practitioner asks the economist, 'What is to be done?' A pure theorist may feel he is not competent to advise since what is to be done in a specific situation is never a simple corollary of theoretical conclusions. It is well known that economists themselves differ even on technical issues. There is the problem of facts with reference to which theories have to be considered and prescriptions for action formed.

As Sir Alec Cairncross, a former Chief Economic Adviser to the UK Treasury put it in the Richard T. Ely Lecture (1985), 'The facts are usually obscure, disputed, seen through different eyes against a different experience of life and stretching far beyond the limited economic context within which the economist seeks to analyze them.'

The theorist is in control of his starting point and is free to make his own assumptions on it. The focus of the practitioner is relatively more specific. Apart from the possible delays in getting data, one has to reckon with the rewriting of the preliminary estimates into final estimates.

In a way, for the practitioner, particularly in India, on a real-time basis, not merely the future but even the past is uncertain. So some approximations or judgements become inevitable. Economic relationships keep changing, and in recent years they are changing faster than ever before.

We are described as 'argumentative Indians'. But, what are we arguing about? Are they the most important and urgent? How do we divide our time and energy between measuring poverty and doing something about it?

There is also the issue of non-economic factors—particularly, institutional and legal factors. The practitioner of public policy has to weigh the political consequences of alternative policy actions, and their timing. For an economist, appeal of economic reform is self-evident but a practitioner of public policy has to be convinced that good economics is also good politics. It is in that context that the exposition of good economics by a practitioner is of exceptional value.

Practitioners of public policy in India have written memoirs more as an explanation, if not in defense, of the events in the past, than as an agenda for debate. Mr Palaniappan Chidambaram has been unique among them in expressing his opinions on a range of burning issues of contemporary importance in a systematic and coherent manner whenever he had a window of opportunity of being out of public office. This volume, a collection of essays, is his second book of this genre.

This collection of essays suggests a list of subjects that require our attention, the issues that need to be deliberated, and the policy alternatives that ought to be considered. They reflect, despite inevitable political bias, Mr Chidambaram's clarity of expression, mastery over detail, command over data, and understanding of electoral politics as well as institutional dynamics in reconciling the desirable, the feasible and the purposeful. They provide clues to the complex links between economics and politics—something that only an intelligent insider to both can appreciate, but will be expressed freely only when he happens to become an outsider.

While there could be many views on the subjects discussed in the volume, Mr Chidambaram brings forth his admirable skills to persuade the reader. For my part, I benefit from reading what he writes, just as I learnt many things in my interactions with him in the past, as assistant, as adviser, and as a member of the team in the practice of public policy.

This volume commends itself for its treatment of contemporary issues drawing from Mr Chidambaram's extensive experience of over three decades in national politics and high-level economic policy-making. Bon aperitif.

6 February 2016

FOREWORD

Montek Singh Ahluwalia
former Deputy Chairman, Planning Commission, Government of India

P. Chidambaram has played a stellar role in Indian politics and policy-making. It has been a privilege for me to work with him in different capacities over the past twenty-five years. Over these years, I have seen for myself his first-rate, razor-sharp mind and his extraordinary capacity to master complex issues, going into minute details of all aspects of a problem, while keeping the larger picture constantly in mind. He also has the rare ability to balance multiple, and at times conflicting issues—social, political and economic—which is an essential requirement for a politician in a vibrant and plural democracy such as ours. Having done the balancing, Chidambaram also has the capacity to come to a firm decision, to own it fully, and then defend and explain the decision to those unconvinced, whether in Parliament or outside.

Chidambaram once said to me that by sitting in Delhi one cannot fathom how government schemes actually worked in the field and how they were viewed by those for whom they were designed. He invited me to accompany him on a day's tour of his constituency, Sivaganga, to get a first-hand exposure. The tour gave me a new perspective. I also got to appreciate how demanding it was for him to serve as Finance Minister and also be a conscientious MP, visiting his remote constituency as often as he did. Getting to Sivaganga involved a three-hour journey by air from Delhi to Chennai, followed by an hour by plane to Madurai, and then several hours of touring by car. He had to do this over the weekend before returning to a mountain of files which he usually cleared in record time.

Since he lived politics and policy when in office, my wife Isher was curious to know how he spent his time when he was not an MP during the term of the first NDA government. He replied that a period out of office was actually very valuable for a politician, because it provided an opportunity to rethink stated positions, and especially reflect on why so many well-intentioned policies often failed to deliver. In his last stint out of office, he wrote a series of columns in the *Indian Express* that were later published as a book. Writing for a newspaper has its own benefits, providing a vehicle for a broader dissemination of ideas and also testing out new ideas. This is his second volume of collected columns written over twelve months in 2015.

The 51 articles published here cover a wide range of subjects including governance, the economy, policy and programs, politics, legislation and foreign policy. As a leading member of the Congress Party, Chidambaram is obviously not writing from a politically neutral perspective, but these columns are also not written as an official party spokesperson. There is no political posturing and grandstanding, both of which have a legitimate role in the theatre of politics, especially in the cut and thrust of parliamentary debate, or on election platforms. Instead, we have a series of highly readable columns, of about 900 words each, dealing with issues that were topical at the time of writing, and many of which remain so even today.

Parliamentary democracy is an adversarial form of government, and it is the job of the Opposition to oppose and criticize. Parliamentary debates should normally provide many opportunities for such issues to be raised by members of the Opposition, and responded to by the Treasury Benches, leaving it to citizens to weigh the issues involved and make up their own minds. It is unfortunate that Parliament has provided too few opportunities for such discussion. The concerned citizen wanting to follow events of importance is forced to watch TV programs, but TV anchors, driven by the relentless search for eyeballs, have given up on the objective of providing an opportunity for reasoned debate. We have to make do with programs where the screen is partitioned into six, or at times even eight, boxes each containing a different talking head, with several of them often talking at the same time at ever rising decibel levels! The only messages that come through are the breaking news tickers at the bottom, which successfully convey news of the most recent developments without interruption.

In this somewhat dysfunctional background of public discussion, the print media becomes the only platform for calm and reasoned discourse. We have many respected columnists who perform this function. Chidambaram's columns add the voice of a seasoned politician who has had vast experience in key positions and who can speak with authority on complex issues. His razor-sharp mind comes through and he writes with rare simplicity and even rarer brevity.

I have mentioned above that in a Parliamentary democracy it is the job of the Opposition to criticize, and this is a job that should be welcomed by all. Inevitably, criticism often involves politicians taking purely political positions, and this too is necessary and beneficial. However, the most productive type of criticism is both constructive and educative. Chidambaram's articles amply meet both tests: they are constructively critical in the sense of providing potential solutions and they are also educative. Let me offer a few examples.

The article on the GST ('History in the Making: The GST Bill') remains topical today. It is to the credit of our democracy that this widely-acclaimed step has now gained very broad bi-partisan support, though some residual problems await resolution. Chidambaram as Finance Minister had much to do in shaping the details of the legislation, which was ultimately introduced by Finance Minister Pranab Mukherjee in March 2011. Chidambaram's article makes specific suggestions on how to resolve the issues that are still contentious.

Another example of constructive criticism with specific solutions offered is the article on the Armed Forces (Special Powers) Act ('Even to the Causing of Death'). Chidambaram says that this legislation, applicable only to the North East and later extended to J&K, gives drastic and unjustified powers not just to the Army but also the central armed police forces. He is clearly not making political capital when he makes a frank admission of his inability to get a consensus within the UPA for amending the Act. He then adds, for concerned citizens to ponder over, that if there is one action which could bring about a dramatic change from J&K to Manipur, it is the repeal of AFSPA and its replacement by a more humane law.

An example of an educative essay is the one on transfers to states ('Equity Suffers a Rs 75,000-crore blow'). Chidambaram explains that the implementation of the Finance Commission recommendations has led to a large increase in the share of central taxes unconditionally transferred to the states. However, this has been offset by a reduction in the resources that earlier used to be transferred via the Planning Commission and Central ministries in the form of Plan assistance and various centrally-sponsored schemes. The states now have more unconditional resources which they can spend on whatever they want. That is precisely what the states, and those in favour of federalism, wanted. As Chidambaram points out, the process of slimming down centrally-sponsored schemes and reducing their conditionality was begun under the UPA. It has been carried further by the NDA accepting the recommendations of the Finance Commission. Chidambaram also says he supports the change, but he draws attention to the fact that there is no way of ensuring that the states spend the money on the areas seen as priority by the Centre. This raises the issue: should the Centre limit itself to trying to persuade the states to spend on areas which it regards as priority or should it generate new centrally-sponsored schemes to fill the gaps? It may well come to this, but isn't that a movie we have seen before? Chidambaram doesn't offer a specific solution, but the article leaves the interested reader much better educated.

Yet another highly educative article is 'What Is Economic Reform, What Is Not'. Every budget speech year after year has had a long list of new initiatives, and these are often referred to as reforms. Chidambaram argues that these are not reforms. He would restrict the term reforms to action which 'makes a clean break from the past, replaces the old with the new, and lays out a new model or a new path'. The article lists 11 actions taken after 1991 that meet the test of genuine reform. I recommend this article to all readers, and especially to students of economics.

I hope more politicians follow Chidambaram's example and take to the print media to share their views on important issues when not in office. It will help them to rethink their own positions afresh. It will also vastly enrich our public discourse. Finally, it will enable the public to hold them to the promises and positions which they espouse when not burdened by the compulsions of high office.

7 February 2016

INTRODUCTION

There is always a first time. My first time with publishing a collection of my columns was in 2006. Those columns had been written between 2001 and 2004 when I was not a member of Parliament and was enjoying a kind of sabbatical from national politics. *A View from the Outside: Why Good Economics Works for Everyone* was essentially an outsider's point of view. Although I had been a minister in several governments and had held different portfolios, my first tenure in the Ministry of Finance was relatively short—June 1996 to March 1998. It was, however, that stint which gave me a unique perspective on governance, especially on matters relating to the economy. I wrote my column as an outsider taking a critical look at the manner in which the country was being governed.

Besides, during 2001 to 2004, my political status was 'independent'. While many saw me as a Congressman—and I did so myself—I was not officially in the Congress party. The bulk of the Congressmen and women in Tamil Nadu, including me, had broken away in 1996 to form a state party. Perhaps, for that reason, my columns were regarded as those of an unattached and relatively independent columnist.

It was only a matter of time before those of us who had separated from the Congress party returned to its fold. Events unfolded in quick succession. I returned on the eve of the Lok Sabha election in April-May 2004, was nominated as the official Congress candidate from my old constituency, Sivaganga, and won comfortably. Within days I found myself in the Cabinet as the Minister of Finance.

NOT ACCORDING TO PLAN

I must confess that I had not planned it that way. I was very pleased to contest the election as a Congress candidate and looked forward to being an active member of Parliament while pursuing other interests—writing, travel and my practice of law which was quite substantial.

There is an interesting story on the sidelines of the formation of the new government. I attended the meeting of the Congress Parliamentary Party (CPP) that elected Ms Sonia Gandhi as the leader and, that night, I left for London to begin an arbitration case for which dates had been set earlier. While in London, we got the news that Ms Gandhi was reluctant to take over as Prime Minister and had called a meeting of the CPP to elect another leader. The buzz was that Dr Manmohan Singh would be elected leader and appointed as the new Prime Minister.

When the date of the CPP meeting was announced, I had no choice but to rush back. I sought an adjournment of two days from the arbitral tribunal. None of the three arbitrators—all retired Indian judges—was convinced that I would return in two days. Mr Harish Salve, my worthy opponent, even declared that I was 'lost' forever and I would become a minister in the new government!

'Minister in the new government' was the last thing on my mind. I had been away from the Congress party for nearly eight years and I had returned, literally, on the eve of the election. Anyway, I got a short adjournment and returned to Delhi. The meeting of the CPP on 18 May 2004 was a turbulent affair. Eventually, Ms Gandhi had her way and stepped aside, and Dr Singh was elected as the leader. After the meeting, I met Dr Singh for a fleeting moment and offered him my congratulations. He asked me to stop by at his residence the next day. I took it as a suggestion to make a purely courtesy call.

The next day was both ordinary and eventful. I called on Dr Singh at his residence at 19 Safdarjung Road (which later became my official residence for ten years) and offered him, once again, my congratulations and good wishes. Dr Singh is a man of few words and, on that day too, spoke very little. He said that he needed everybody's help, including mine.

I responded that, of course, he would certainly get everybody's help. The meeting was turning out to be a routine one until Dr Singh asked me to stay back in Delhi and meet him again. Alarm bells began to ring in my head!

I had no choice but to request the arbitrators to defer the hearing once again, and they kindly obliged. I stayed back in Delhi. I got a call from Ms Gandhi and Dr Singh and was sworn in as a minister on 22 May 2004. The expectation was that the Prime Minister would keep the Finance portfolio with himself. Besides, there were many deserving claimants for Finance, including several economists. I expected to be given Commerce, my last portfolio in a Congress government. I do not know until this day how or why the portfolio of Finance was assigned to me. I served as Finance Minister in two spells; in between I served as Home Minister for three years and eight months.

INVENTING A ROLE

After Mr Narendra Modi's government took office in May 2014 and I returned to private life, I decided to resume my weekly column. My position was very different from what it was in 2001. I had served ten years in two of the most important ministries of the government—Finance and Home. I was among the most recognized faces of the United Progressive Alliance (UPA) governments. I had received more than my fair share of bouquets and brickbats! I was duly warned that nothing that I said or wrote would go unnoticed or uncommented. Besides, there would be a constant reference to what I had said or done when I had been a minister. In short, it was clear that I would not be the average columnist and every word that I wrote would come under close scrutiny.

It was indeed a challenge and I accepted it. After exploring a few options, I returned to my favourite platform, the *Indian Express*. Although my friend and editor (during 2001 to 2004), Mr Shekhar Gupta, had left the newspaper, the new Editor, Mr Rajkamal Jha, and the editorial board were very welcoming and enthusiastic.

The choice of the title for the column was deliberate. We decided to call it 'Across the Aisle'. That firmly placed me in the ranks of the Opposition (to the government). That is where I belong as a member of the Congress party. It is also consistent with my political and economic views which I believe are secular, liberal and in favour of an open and competitive economy—and quite the opposite of what Mr Narendra Modi's government stands for. I reject the notion of a 'loyal' Opposition; I am part of the true (but not disloyal) Opposition in a plural democracy. The Opposition's task in a parliamentary democracy is to 'oppose, expose and depose' the government of the day. There are many columnists who support the government and that is their right. My role is to be firmly 'across the aisle'—the place assigned to the Opposition.

I have taken my role seriously, but many voices in the social media do not seem to understand the need for, and the role of, the Opposition. I write based on solid research and after deep reflection. I choose my words carefully. I do not use harsh or discourteous language and have never resorted to abuse or calumny. Since I am no longer a member of Parliament, the column was my platform to speak on matters that I believed were fit to be raised in Parliament or for public debate.

I can claim that I have been one of the few regular, consistent and reasoned voices of opposition to the government for over one year. To my pleasant surprise, I found that, on a few issues, I contributed to formulating the policy of the Congress party—on the ill-conceived ordinance to amend the Land Acquisition, Rehabilitation and Resettlement Act and on the Goods and Services Tax Bill.

I chose my subject depending upon what was topical or relevant. Usually, the subject concerned the economy or the budget or one of the policies or programmes of the government. Many columns dealt with contemporary political issues and issues of governance. Looking back, I find that the poor management of the economy, the rise of intolerance, and the majoritarian approach of the National Democratic Alliance (NDA) government and the Bharatiya Janata Party (BJP) were recurring themes.

You will find that I was bemused when the government did U-turns on a number of issues. I was anguished that we had learnt and had forgotten the lessons of the past. I was concerned by the government's failure to read the economic trends. I was happy to see once-rubbished programmes become flagship projects under the new government. I was appalled by the level of public discourse involving ministers and MPs. I was outraged by the rash of bans. I was devastated when Rohith Vemula committed suicide. Writing every week was an outlet for my strongly-held beliefs and views. I tried my best to capture the state of the country as I saw it that week. At the end of the year I was happy that I did not skip a single week in the 51 weeks beginning 11 January 2015.

I received a lot of feedback. Friends brought to my notice the reactions expressed through the social media. Frequently, there would be a heartwarming comment from an unexpected quarter or a complete stranger. Regardless of the praise or the criticism, I was delighted to know that the column was widely read. That alone was sufficient reward, and the belief that the essays will be read more widely has led me to agree to publish this collection.

IS HUMOUR DEAD?

Did I learn anything to my regret through the year 2015? Yes, and it is that humour is dead in public discourse in India. People don't laugh enough—at themselves and at or with others. We don't seem to know what satire is. Two columns—written as satire—triggered a torrent of abuse from a section of the readers. An open letter to the Prime Minister written by a fictional 'average citizen' provoked a distinguished author and journalist to argue, in an angry rebuttal, that I was not an average citizen!

I continue to write my column in 2016. Writing is, first and foremost, an act of self-discipline. It forces one to think, gather authentic information, reflect, and then express oneself precisely. If people read what I write that is reward enough; they do not have to agree with me. The reward will be even greater if my writing is able to influence people, alter policy, and bring about a change for the better.

Sitting across the aisle, I do not become an enemy of anyone, and certainly not an enemy of the government. I do not lose my right to claim that I love my country, that I cherish my principles and beliefs, and that the purpose of my writing is to influence people and their thought and behaviour. This collection is intended to enlarge the circle of regular readers. If you have the book in your hand, I want you to be part of that circle.

Now, go ahead, and read the book. It is for you to decide whether I have succeeded in describing accurately the state of the nation in 2015.

THE BEGINNING AND THE END

THE STATE OF THE UNION 2015

11 January 2015

I am happy to be back in this space and begin a conversation.

Before and during the election to the Lok Sabha, we were concerned with the state of the economy. After the election, and seven months after a new government assumed office, those concerns have not gone away. Rather, new questions concerning the economy and the polity are being raised every day.

In the middle of 2013, the economy was on the mend. Then, Mr Ben Bernanke struck with a thoughtless remark on withdrawing from 'quantitative easing', when that step was several months away. Nevertheless, the government of the day gamely stuck to the target of fiscal deficit, contained the current account deficit, allocated money for public investment and key social sector programmes, and promised that economic growth would revive in 2014–15.

Calendar 2014 can be divided nearly equally between the United Progressive Alliance (UPA) government and the National Democratic Alliance (NDA) government. Luckily, therefore, we do not have to apportion blame or deny credit.

THE ECONOMY

One year ago, growth was faltering and the financial year ended with an unsatisfactory 4.7 per cent.* Today, after 5.7 per cent and 5.3 per cent in Q1 and Q2 of 2014–15, there is still no assurance of revival.

At the end of November 2013, year-on-year non-food credit growth was 14.7 per cent; at the end of November 2014 it was just 11 per cent.

The decline in the rate of inflation began in November 2013 (see graph) when the UPA was in office. Thirteen months later, the decline continues, accelerated by the fall in the price of crude oil, a windfall for the NDA.

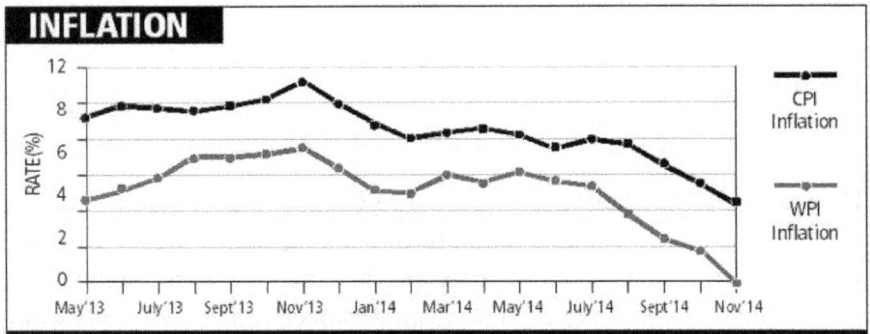

Last year, at this time, the price of Brent crude oil was around US$ 99 per barrel. This year it is around US$ 53 per barrel, and falling. The government has been able to play both good cop and bad cop. It has cut prices of petrol and diesel as well as raised duties on petrol and diesel.

At end-2013, the repo rate (set by the Reserve Bank of India [RBI]) was 7.75 per cent. At end-2014, it stood at 8 per cent. Then, the rupee had traded at 61.90 to the dollar; now it is at 63.33. A year ago, RBI's foreign currency assets (FCA) stood at US$ 268 billion; this year has begun with an impressive US$ 295 billion. Prime Minister Modi is a votary of a 'strong' rupee—his party had argued for Rs 40 to the dollar—but the RBI is happy to see a gradual depreciation! I am pretty certain that the RBI is buying dollars and letting the rupee slide. Mr Modi and the rupee are trending together—one crossing, other touching, 64.

On 1 January 2014, I was upset that the Bharatiya Janata Party (BJP)

---

*It has since been revised to 6.6 per cent as per the new GDP definition.

had blocked the Insurance Laws (Amendment) Bill, 2008, and I did not have the numbers to promulgate an ordinance or threaten to call a joint session of both Houses to pass the Bill. On 1 January 2015, Mr Jaitley was upset that the opposition in the Rajya Sabha had blocked the Insurance Laws (Amendment) Bill, 2008 and, therefore, he has used his numbers to promulgate an ordinance and has threatened to call, if need be, a joint session of both Houses to pass the Bill.

On 1 January 2014, I gave up on the hope of persuading the states of Gujarat, Madhya Pradesh and Tamil Nadu to come on board to get Goods and Services Tax (GST) started. I left behind a draft of the Constitution Amendment Bill and an incomplete draft of the GST Bill. On 1 January 2015, Mr Jaitley nursed the hope that the states of Gujarat, Madhya Pradesh and Tamil Nadu will come on board to get GST started.

In 2014, 'Aadhaar' was rubbished and Mr Nilekani was fighting an election. In 2015, 'Aadhaar' reigns and Mr Nilekani is forgotten.

THE POLITY

Just before the start of 2014, the idea of a National Counter Terrorism Centre (NCTC) was foolishly scuttled by non-Congress state governments. Just before the start of 2015, a non-Congress central government has wisely discovered the need for a NCTC. In early 2014, the National Intelligence Grid (NATGRID) was tottering because of opposition of the Intelligence Bureau (IB) and insufficient support of the Ministry of Home Affairs. Towards the end of 2014, NATGRID was on a trot with an IB officer as its head and enthusiastic support of the Prime Minister's Office.

At the dawn of 2014, the International Border and the Line of Control between India and Pakistan were relatively quiet. At the dawn of 2015, the India–Pakistan border is one of the hottest borders. 2014 witnessed over 500 ceasefire violations. About 40 security personnel were killed or injured in firing, 113 villages were evacuated, and about 30,000 persons were displaced from their homes.

One year ago, the words that resonated through the length and breadth of the country were development, investment and jobs. Today, the phrases that dominate public discourse are 'ghar wapsi' (reconversion), 'love jihad' (love conquest) and 'Ramzaada vs haramzaada' (Ram's children vs bastards).

2014 was the year of acrimony. 2015 promises to be the year of acronyms.

2014 began with the message 'Mr Modi can deliver'. 2015 has begun with the question 'Can Mr Modi deliver?'

CONFESSIONS OF A STRICKEN CONSCIENCE

27 December 2015

The truth is out, finally.

I began this weekly column in January 2015 with a piece on the state of the Union. I have been saved the trouble of making a year-end assessment. That job has been performed admirably by the Economic Division of the Department of Economic Affairs, Ministry of Finance, Government of India. Thank god, we have always allowed them the autonomy and freedom to produce the annual Economic Survey as well as the mid-year Economic Analysis.

The mid-year Analysis for 2015–16 presented last week contains a string of confessions and admissions that tell us more about the Narendra Modi government's performance than all the learned commentaries taken together. Here are some.

UPA YEARS WERE BOOM YEARS

'We undertake this analysis for three time periods: the boom years, from 2004–05 to 2011–12, 2014–15 and the first half of 2015–16. The striking finding about this year is that compared to the past, the Indian economy is now powered by private consumption and government investment. This is in sharp contrast to the boom years, when the economy was powered by all four components of demand.'

The admission is that private investment and exports are languishing. It is like a car running on two wheels.

There is another related confession: 'In the boom years, exports were adding 1.9 percentage points to demand whereas in 2015–16 export demand has been falling (–1.1 percentage points). Similarly, private investment contributed 3.2 percentage points (in the boom years) and only 1 percentage point in the current year.'

PRIVATE SECTOR UNDER STRESS

For a government that is believed to be pro-business, and had the support of big business and big money, its biggest failure is the moribund state of the private sector.

The Analysis confesses, 'Why is private investment weak? Corporate balance sheets remain highly stressed... the weighted average interest cover ratio has declined from 2.5 in September 2014 to 2.3 in September 2015... a rise in the indebtedness is reflected in a rise in the debt to EBIDTA ratio from 2.8 to 2.9 over the same period. Profit after tax for the corporate sector as a whole has remained largely flat in FY 2015 vis-à-vis FY 2014. As a result, capital expenditures as a share of GDP have declined further from 5.4 to 5.2 per cent of GDP.'

There are more tell-tale signs. In June–September 2015, net sales of firms fell by 5.3 per cent compared to the same period last year. The outlook for the manufacturing sector is particularly bleak with net sales down 12 per cent. Non-food credit is growing at 8.3 per cent, the slowest in 20 years. Growth of credit to industry is 4.6 per cent while credit to medium enterprises actually shrunk by 9.1 per cent.

CAUSES OF RURAL DISTRESS

The Analysis confesses, 'Rural wage growth and minimum support price increases—important determinants of inflation—have remained muted'. Both flow out of explicit and deliberate policy decisions of the government. The monsoon has added to the woes of farmers. As the Analysis points out, 'Latest data for the rabi season suggests that net sown area is lower than for the corresponding period of last year; this combined with the likely adverse productivity effects from four consecutive seasons of weak rainfall create downside risks to agricultural production for this fiscal year.' Correlate these to the number of suicides by farmers that are reported. Such are the consequences of the absence of a coherent policy for the farm sector and will also explain why there is so much rural distress and angst.

WHERE ARE THE PROMISED JOBS?

'Where are the jobs?' is the question uppermost in the minds of most persons and most families. The 26th quarterly employment survey conducted between April and June 2015 showed that job creation in the manufacturing and export-oriented sectors fell by a net of 43,000 from the previous quarter. This is the worst performance in six years. In the same quarter of 2014, these sectors had added 182,000 jobs. The Analysis is silent on job creation. The silence itself is a confession.

FISCAL DEFICIT A CHALLENGE

The most worrisome confession is that 'The decline in nominal GDP growth relative to the budget assumption will pose a challenge for meeting the fiscal deficit target of 3.9 per cent of GDP. Slower-than-anticipated nominal GDP growth (8.2 per cent versus budget estimate of 11.5) will itself raise the deficit target by 0.2 per cent of GDP.'

Nevertheless, I believe that the government will meet the target of 3.9 per cent this year, but what about the next fiscal year? There is an ominous warning: 'If the government sticks to the path for fiscal consolidation, that would further detract from demand. On these assumptions, and unless supply-side reforms provide an impetus to growth, real Gross Domestic Product (GDP) growth next year based on an analysis of likely demand is not likely to be significantly greater than growth this year.'

So, we have been warned.

ACHCHE DIN FAR AWAY

Since nominal GDP growth in the second quarter was only 6 per cent, the estimated nominal GDP growth of 8.2 per cent for FY 2015–16 as a whole is a 'pie in the sky'. The estimate of real GDP growth for the year at 7–7.5 per cent range safely assumes a much lower point. Wisely, the Analysis makes no claim for GDP growth in 2016–17 and there is no boast of achieving 8 per cent plus growth rates!

The achche din bells have fallen silent.

GOVERNANCE

WILL THE CAMPAIGN END AFTER R-DAY?

25 January 2015

In some ways, India is beginning to look like the United States. For example, take our elections. On running an election campaign, Mr Barack Obama was a master. Mr Narendra Modi was a quick learner. Never before 2014 did India's election to the Lok Sabha witness such a masterly combination of organization, money and technology (that cost, as the BJP officially reported, Rs 487 crore). It resembled a US presidential election.

A US president never ceases to run. He is a perennial campaigner. He has no choice. The US House of Representatives is elected every two years. No sooner is the winner declared on election day in November than he or she is running for re-election barely two years away. If a US president wishes to keep control of his legislative agenda, he must ensure that his party keeps control of the House of Representatives. So, a US president is continuously on the campaign trail.

India's elections are held once in five years. For a few decades, elections to the Lok Sabha and to state legislative assemblies were held together. That changed in the 1970s.

The norm for election to the Lok Sabha is once in five years (the exceptions were 1977/1980, 1989/1991, and 1996/1998/1999). Prime Ministers seldom campaigned in state elections and hence were not seen constantly on the campaign trail. That has changed with the arrival of Mr Modi.

IN CAMPAIGN MODE

Since his name was announced in September 2013 as the BJP's candidate for prime minister, Mr Modi has been on the campaign trail. Credit is due to Mr Modi for being an indefatigable campaigner—whether in an Indian city or Kathmandu or New York or Tokyo or Sydney. Every speech of Mr Modi—whether to scientists or students, bankers or businesspersons—is a campaign speech. He is perpetually wooing his audience to vote for his party at whatever election that is round the corner!

Mr Modi's foreign travels are no different. They have little to do with foreign policy and have less to show in terms of foreign policy achievements. The target audience (beyond the assembly of persons of Indian origin) is always the domestic constituency.

Prime Minister Modi's major engagements with foreign leaders in the last eight months have been with the heads of government of Japan, Australia, Russia, China and the United States.

Let us make an objective assessment of the outcomes of those engagements.

THE WISH LIST GROWS

Despite Mr Vajpayee's and Dr Manmohan Singh's attempts to instil a strategic dimension, India–US relations have, for the most part, been transactional. Mr Modi's efforts have not yet produced a transaction equal to the Civil Nuclear Agreement between the two countries. Even that agreement has not resulted in commercial cooperation because of the liability clause which the BJP and others vociferously demanded. There is a yawning gap between the two countries on a number of matters including US aid to Pakistan, the balance of power in Asia, climate change, transfer of defence technology, access to David Headley, the IPR 'priority watch list', the Bilateral Investment Treaty, solar panel imports, and the totalization agreement.

There have not been major takeaways from the engagements with other countries as well. The Tokyo Declaration after Mr Modi's visit repeatedly used the word 'dialogue'. There was no agreement on civil nuclear cooperation or the US-2 amphibian aircraft or the Shinkansen rail.

Mr Abbott came with a clear objective: to sell Australian uranium. And he left with a concrete agreement: on Cooperation in the Peaceful Uses of Nuclear Energy. The more important Comprehensive Economic Cooperation Agreement is still some distance away.

The joint statement after Mr Putin's visit—the high-sounding Druzhba-Dosti—was a long wish list, but contained no concrete agreements. There was no agreement on the price of nuclear reactors to be erected at Kudankulam and at a site yet to be identified.

PLAYING CHINESE CHECKERS

The most intriguing joint statement was the one issued after Mr Xi Jinping's visit in the middle of September 2014. It was a State visit in a literal sense—to the state of Gujarat—with a stopover in Delhi on the way back home. The only agreement was on the announcement of the establishment of two industrial parks, one in Gujarat and the other in Maharashtra (where the election date was 15 October). As the two leaders sat on a jhoola, and it was confirmed that nearly 1,000 Chinese troops had intruded five kilometres in the Chumur sector, the officials of both sides were hammering out a statement that pledged 'to seek a fair, reasonable and mutually acceptable solution' to the India–China boundary question. A date could not be set for a meeting of the Special Representatives.

Engaging foreign leaders and countries requires clarity, strategy and patience. President Obama's visit may turn out to be a strategic outreach or a well-deserved family outing. We must watch for the outcomes. The dazzle of the Obama engagement may swing a few votes the BJP's way in the Delhi election but, sooner than later, the Prime Minister must get off the campaign bandwagon and deliver on his engagements with foreign governments and promises to the people.

THE BUGLE HAS BEEN SOUNDED

19 April 2015

In a column that was published in the *Indian Express* on 22 March 2015 ('Equity suffers Rs 75,000-crore blow'), I had pointed out that central assistance to state Plan(s) had been reduced by more than Rs 75,000 crore in the budget for 2015–16 from the assistance in the revised budget of 2014–15. If one compared the budget estimate for 2014–15 and the budget estimate for 2015–16, the reduction was extremely harsh—nearly Rs 135,000 crore.

After the Fourteenth Finance Commission, it is nobody's case that no cuts were warranted. The key question was 'which schemes could be best designed and funded by the state governments and which schemes would still need the lead and financial support of the central government'? That question was not asked and hence the Procrustean cuts.

IMPACT ON POLICE MODERNISATION

The more worrisome question is 'what will be the qualitative impact of the cuts'? Will not the cut in expenditure impact, adversely, some vital aspects of the scheme? The answer is self-evident: it will affect critical inputs or coverage or spread or duration of the scheme and, in an extreme case, prompt its burial. As more people become aware of the baneful consequences of such reduction, more voices are being raised, both within and outside the government.

One of the centrally-sponsored schemes that the budget has delinked from central support is the National Scheme for Modernisation of Police and Other Forces. In 2014–15 (RE), Rs 1,433 crore was provided as assistance; this year it is nil and, hereafter, the states have to find the money. The ostensible reason for the change of policy is that 'law and order' is a state subject.

It is common knowledge that there are critical gaps in the state police structure—number of policemen and women, vehicles, weapons, communication equipment, forensic laboratories, training centres, anti-terrorist, counter insurgency and other special forces, canine squads, crime records, etc. Besides, there is an inter-state aspect to policing. Criminals, especially terrorists, do not respect state borders. Police infrastructure along state borders and along the coast is a critical need. It is funding that gave the central government oversight on these matters and the vital responsibility of coordination.

THE IDEA OF CCTNS

Another problem in policing was that the police of one state barely 'talked' among themselves or to the police of another state. Each police station was an island, and records were maintained manually at the police station. The National Crime Records Bureau, followed by the setting up of State Crime Records Bureaus, was the first step towards storage, sharing and accessing data—but it remained technologically primitive and cumbersome. What was required was a seamless, technology-driven network where any police station could 'talk' to another police station on a real-time basis. Hence, the idea of the Crime and Criminal Tracking Network and System (CCTNS) was conceived. It is a system to facilitate collection, storage, retrieval, analysis, transfer and sharing of data and information at the police station, between a police station and another police station or district HQ or state HQ, and between the police of one state and another state or the central government, including the Intelligence Bureau (IB),

Central Bureau of Investigation (CBI) and central police organizations. The system had to overcome problems of hardware, software, security, privilege and, above all, language.

After months of negotiations, training of personnel, handholding, and promise of generous financial assistance, all states were brought on board. The ambitious scheme is being implemented, albeit with some delay. Successful completion will depend upon adequate and timely provision of funds, close monitoring and coordination. The idea is to build a national system, not a collection of 29 state systems. Besides, the system must be upgraded periodically with infusion of new technology, equipment and software. These can be done only if there is an oversight mechanism to ensure that all states—and I mean *all* states—move at the same speed and agree on every aspect of the system.

It is at this crucial juncture that the government has decided to cut off funds to CCTNS. I suspect the decision was one of those routine bureaucratic actions and not much thought went into making the decision at the higher levels of government.

SOUND THE BUGLE

What I have said about CCTNS will apply to some other schemes which have been completely delinked from central funds. The Special Infrastructure Scheme (SIS) for Naxalite-affected areas is an example. I wish Ms Sudha Pillai (former secretary, Planning Commission) or some of the district collectors who implemented SIS during their tenures will speak or write about the transformation brought about by SIS in areas that had been grossly neglected for decades by the state governments concerned.

Thankfully, the Ministry of Home Affairs is not taking the decision to deny funds to Modernisation of Police Forces, CCTNS and SIS without protest. Media reports say that Mr L.C. Goyal, Home Secretary, has written 'multiple letters' to the Ministry of Finance. I presume the letters were written with the approval of Mr Rajnath Singh, Home Minister.

The Home Minister has sounded the first bugle. It is time for the ministers of Health, Human Resource Development, Social Justice and Empowerment, and Women and Child Development to protest the denial or drastic reduction of funds to critical national schemes under their charge.

LETTER TO THE PRIME MINISTER

31 May 2015

Dear Mr Prime Minister,

I am an average citizen. I belong to an average family, had an average education, live in an average town, hold an average job, and have average ambitions. I am aware that because I am the son of a school teacher, hold a bachelor's degree (second class) and have a job, I may actually be above the average. It only shows how low the average is.

In the last week, my fellow citizens and I have been bombarded with editorials, columns, statements, interviews, blogs, tweets and what not, and I am quite confused. I thought your letter of 26 May that appeared in all the newspapers would put things in perspective but, I am afraid, it has left me more confused. So, please bear with me while I ask you a few questions.

WHERE ARE THE JOBS?

My first question is, how is the economy doing? To me and my children, and to all families on our street, the most important concern is jobs. Will you please tell us the number of jobs that were created in the first year of your government? The numbers I have seen are a little over one lakh of jobs every quarter, so that makes a grand total of four to five lakh jobs in the whole year. I also read that there are 85 lakh persons registered with the employment exchanges in Tamil Nadu. If we extrapolate that number for the whole country, don't you agree that the situation is alarming? So, please tell us the truth about jobs.

That takes me to the next question, who is creating the jobs? My neighbour who teaches economics in the local government college told me that no real new jobs can be created in farming. She thinks that only if more people start new businesses, and more large plants are built to produce power or steel or cars or mobile phones or anything, will there be more direct and indirect jobs. She said the key word is investment and encouraged me to ask you what were the amounts invested in the last year by the public sector enterprises and the private sector, what is the number of jobs they expect to add once the projects go into production, and when. By the way, why don't we see advertisements of a bhumi puja or an inauguration of a big project costing a few thousand crore rupees as we used to do a few years ago?

WHY IS EVERYONE CONCERNED?

A relative of mine who runs a small business told me that banks are loath to give loans. Dr Rangarajan, in a recent article, said that hundreds of public and private projects are stalled. A journalist told me that electricity consumption in the country has remained flat in the last five months. Companies producing consumer goods say that 'aggregate demand' is depressed, which I don't understand, but I am sure you do. I heard a lawyer say on television that every major company in the power, coal, oil & gas, airport, road, telecommunications and pharmaceutical sectors is embroiled in litigation. If this is the actual situation, Mr Prime Minister, how do you expect a foreign investor, or for that matter an Indian investor, to invest in India?

The excuse of the Finance Minister is 'these are legacy issues', but, to my simple mind, that is the lot of every government. Every government will inherit a set of problems and must resolve them. Let me remind you that you were voted to power on the promise of replicating the Gujarat model (whatever that was, I don't know) and the promise of achche din.

There is no room for excuses.

I am worried about the massive cuts in the funds allocated to health, education, mid-day meal scheme, drinking water, Integrated Child Development Scheme (ICDS), Rashtriya Krishi Vikas Yojana (RKVY) and SC & ST welfare. I read that chief ministers have complained and now some of your ministers are complaining. I am told the consequences will be felt by the end of the year.

WHY IS SO MUCH ENERGY WASTED ON DIVISIVE ISSUES?

Other anecdotal evidence has put fear in the minds of the people and eroded trust in the government. A graduate is denied a job and a working lady is evicted from her rented flat because they are Muslims. Mr Julio Ribeiro expresses his anguish at the rise of intolerance against minorities, non-governmental organizations (NGOs), and civil society activists. BJP governments in states ban the sale or consumption of beef. Can you really ban anything in an open society and a connected world and, even if you can, how many things will you ban—meat, books, foreign travel, documentaries, swear words in films, NGOs?

My last question is, what are you doing with the absolute majority that we gave your party in the elections? Some of your MPs are an embarrassment. (So was your statement on 'sinning and being born Indian' that you made in Seoul.) I thought you will use your mandate to bring about a transformation in policies, programmes and implementation, but what I see is centralization of authority in your hands and more talk than action. *The Economist* has described you as a One-Man Band who needs a new tune. I hope you will listen to your critics, who also have the country's welfare and progress at heart.

Yours sincerely,
A concerned citizen

A GREEK TRAGEDY EVERY WHICH WAY

12 July 2015

Greece is not a rogue state. It does not harbour terrorist groups. It has no territorial ambitions. Greece is a lovely country that boasts of one of the oldest civilizations of the world and is proud of its contributions to mathematics, philosophy and statecraft. Greece's connection with India began with a young warrior-king, Alexander. When the reigning king visited India in the early 1960s, President Radhakrishnan is reported to have greeted him with the words, 'Your Majesty is the first King of Greece to visit India—invited!'

Greece has fallen on evil days because it did something which millions of individuals—and some countries—do: it borrowed more than its capacity to repay. Year after year it ran a high fiscal deficit and a high current account deficit and financed them by borrowing more. Its debt to GDP ratio stands at 150 per cent.

SOURCE OF ALL TROUBLE

Now, I hope, readers will understand why I have argued consistently for containing the twin deficits. They are the source of all trouble. Practically everything can be traced to the level of the deficits: inflation, interest rate, exchange rate, foreign investment, the domestic savings rate and the sovereign's credit rating.

The Greek crisis is essentially about poor macro-economic management. There was a time when capital poured into Greece, but that changed with the global crisis of 2008. The crisis had a particularly severe impact on four European countries: Portugal, Iceland, Greece and Spain.

It had its reverberations elsewhere too, not excluding India, but even if I say it, the fact is that India managed the crisis very well (read a cover story by P. Vaidyanathan Iyer titled 'How they saved the India story' in *Eye*, the Sunday magazine of the *Indian Express*, 26 September 2010).

Undoubtedly, the borrower must take a large share of the blame. The creditors too must take their share. Both exhibited poor judgement. Mr Tsipras expects to be treated honourably because he is the democratically elected leader of a sovereign country. But most lenders are also sovereigns or sovereign-backed central banks. Both sides are playing hard ball. I hope they will eventually agree on a plan that will include a bailout by the lenders and hard and deep reforms by the borrower.

The lenders are stressing on one word: austerity. Austerity is a fine principle, but how much austerity can you impose on a country whose economy has shrunk nearly 30 per cent in the last five years, where 25 per cent of the people are unemployed, and where youth unemployment stands at 50 per cent?

I too have pleaded for austerity. I called it fiscal discipline. When I found that government expenditure had overshot prudent limits for three successive years—and the government was applauded for maintaining a high growth rate thanks to the high expenditure—I persuaded the UPA government to change course. We appointed the Kelkar Committee, got a new fiscal consolidation path, and stuck to it through 2012–13 and 2013–14 in the face of virulent criticism.

On 28 February 2013, I said in the budget speech, 'We must redeem our promise by 2016–17 and bring down the fiscal deficit to 3 per cent, the revenue deficit to 1.5 per cent and the effective revenue deficit to zero.'

AUSTERITY VS DEPRIVATION

It is here that we have an ethical and moral dilemma. We may have lifted 140 million people out of poverty during 2004–2014, but millions of Indians are still poor. The Socio Economic and Caste Census (SECC) has brought out, starkly, the level of deprivation among the people. The picture of rural India is grim. 62 per cent of the 17.91 crore households are deprived. 13.34 crore households (74.5 per cent) have a monthly income of Rs 5,000 or less. 6.86 crore households (38.27 per cent) earn their livelihood through manual casual labour. 2.37 crore households (13.3 per cent) live in one-room kuchcha dwellings. Data for the 6.47 crore households in urban India has not been released.

THREE-FOLD PROBLEMS

In the name of austerity, how long can the State deny funds to tackle the problems of deprivation? How long can the State ask people to wait to have a private toilet or enrol in a good school or find a hospital bed? How long will people wait for clean drinking tap water or an all-weather village road or a decent, secure job? The answer is, not for long, because the anger will boil over.

Our problems are three-fold:

1. lack of adequate funds;
2. lack of a civil service that can deliver outcomes;
3. unwillingness of the better-off classes to shoulder a part of the burden of the government.

Austerity has a connection to the first problem. But even when adequate funds are provided, there is the second problem, that the outcomes are dismal: look at the outcomes of the Clean Ganga project or the RRR project for water bodies or the Accelerated Irrigation Benefit Programme. There have been honourable exceptions—abolition of polio and delivery of education loans. The third problem is the self-absorbed affluent classes which let the country down by refusing to pay their taxes or fulfil the social obligations they have undertaken (e.g. promise to build school toilets).

Austerity for macro-economic stability must be balanced with targeted expenditure to get rid of deprivation. Not often do governments succeed in striking the right balance.

SPEECH IS SILVER, SILENCE GOLDEN

19 July 2015

Who said 'speech is silver, silence golden'? The proverb is attributed to ancient Egypt, to Zen Buddhism and to Thomas Carlyle. A wag claimed that the copyright now belonged to Mr Narendra Modi.

Through the election campaign, I marveled at Mr Modi's ability to work the crowd to a frenzy of support with his mastery over the spoken word. His team came up with clever ideas, hard-hitting arguments and brilliant turns-of-phrase. But it was Mr Modi's oratory that held the crowd spellbound. He seemed to have an answer for everything, nothing fazed him, and towards the end of the campaign, he even took the brave step of granting one-on-one interviews. By that time, of course, he had stitched up a victory.

Mr Modi's style of communication was strictly one way. He spoke, you listened. His points made, he left the stage. No media conferences, no off-the-cuff remarks on the sidelines of an event, no sound bytes. He controlled his communications totally and continued that practice even after becoming Prime Minister.

VOLUBLE AND VERSATILE

But Mr Modi spoke a lot and on a lot of subjects and at a lot of places. As Prime Minister, I believe, he has averaged three or four events a week. He has spoken in India and in 26 countries. He has spoken both in Hindi and in English. He has spoken on many stages, through signed articles, via recorded messages, and through tweets. He has spoken on many subjects—on India's development to India's defence, on Clean India to Vibrant India, on Make in India to Skill India, on global terror to climate change, on yoga to yogis.

He was most eloquent when he spoke on corruption and he warmed up to the subject, like no other, when it concerned the alleged corruption during the 10 years of the UPA government. The Prime Minister was the white knight on a silver steed who had come to Delhi to slay the demon of corruption. In his dictionary, 'corruption' was a catch-all word that took within its fold impropriety, abuse of authority, conflict of interest, black money, bribes, disproportionate assets and virtually anything that carried a whiff of suspicion. In his book, anyone accused by the BJP of corruption was 'presumed guilty until proven otherwise'.

SEE AND HEAR NO EVIL

Alas, all that is a distant memory. Instead, today we have a Prime Minister who will 'see no evil and hear no evil' when it concerns the ministers in his council of ministers or the BJP's chief ministers or ministers or his friends and fellow swayamsevaks. And because he will see no evil or hear no evil, he will not speak on any of them. Mr Modi's new armour is silence, his oratory restricted to re-launching ongoing schemes of the UPA (latest example: the National Skill Development Mission).

When allegations surfaced against him, Mr Lalit Modi fled to London. He was wanted by the Enforcement Directorate for questioning. He did not appear. His passport was revoked by the Ministry of External Affairs (MEA), but he managed to stay on in London. He wanted a travel document to enable him to travel and approached his 'family friend' Ms Sushma Swaraj. She is no longer a mere friend, she is the Minister of External Affairs. She wanted to help him on 'humanitarian grounds'. Ms Swaraj kept the foreign secretary, her ministry and the Indian High Commissioner in the dark, but told the British High Commissioner that India would have no objection if Britain issued Mr Lalit Modi a travel document. Fact is, it was her nudge that got Mr Lalit Modi a travel document that enabled him to travel the whole world—not only to Portugal to be by the side of his ailing wife.

MANY QUESTIONS, NO ANSWERS

On these admitted facts, we asked:
1. Why did the Minister keep everybody in the dark and speak directly to the British High Commissioner? Is it not a case of abuse of authority? Answer: silence.
2. Why did the Minister not advise Mr Lalit Modi to apply to the Indian High Commission in London for a temporary travel document but, instead, spoke to the British High Commissioner on his behalf? Is it not a case of acting 'with favour', otherwise called favouritism or nepotism? Answer: silence.
3. Mr Lalit Modi's counsel in the High Court in the petition against the cancellation of his passport was the Minister's daughter. The respondent was the MEA. Mr Lalit Modi succeeded. The ministry took a decision not to appeal the judgment (or took no decision). In either situation, the result was the same and the judgment became final. Who took the decision (or took no decision) in the MEA? Since the Minister was constructively responsible, was it not her decision? Should not the Minister have recused herself from the matter because her daughter was the counsel for Mr Modi? Is it not a case of conflict of interest? Answer: silence.

The Lalit Modi–Sushma Swaraj story has abuse of authority, nepotism and conflict of interest written all over. By the Prime Minister's earlier silver standard, the case demands the Minister's resignation. But Mr Modi has now switched to the gold standard of silence and hopes that the storm will blow over. Whether it does or does not, it will almost certainly blow away a whole session of Parliament.

SUSHMA SWARAJ, RTI AND A PARLIAMENT QUESTION

26 July 2015

I did not expect to write about the Lalit Modi–Sushma Swaraj controversy again this week. But it is the issue that has dominated media space, public discourse and Parliament for a whole week. Irrespective of the wishes of the Prime Minister and the government, it will not go away.

A news channel broke the story on 14 June 2015. Three days later, I addressed a media conference and read out a statement containing seven questions to the government. The questions could have been answered in a pretty straightforward manner, but that is not the way guilty minds work. No answers were forthcoming and there was deafening silence.

THE RTI REQUEST...

Enter Mr Rayo, a citizen. He copied the seven questions and shot off an RTI (Right to Information) Request on 18 June 2015. The under secretary (RTI), MEA sent a reply on 26 June 2015.

The first three questions sought facts that were within the exclusive knowledge of Ms Sushma Swaraj, the Minister of External Affairs: Why has the government not released the letters exchanged between the Finance

Minister and the UK Chancellor? Why did Ms Swaraj not advise Mr Lalit Modi to apply for a temporary Indian travel document? Why did Ms Swaraj not advise Mr Lalit Modi to return to India first as a condition for issue of a travel document?

It is quite obvious that only Ms Swaraj could have provided answers to these questions. Presumably, she did, and the under secretary replied on behalf of the MEA as under:

'The office of the External Affairs Minister (EAM) has informed that the questions in Serial No. 1 to 3 of your RTI do not seem to fall under the purview of the RTI Act, 2005.'

According to Ms Sushma Swaraj, her conversation with the British High Commissioner and her failure to advise Mr Lalit Modi to return to India and apply for a travel document do not fall within the purview of the RTI Act!

If the audacity of that answer took your breath away, look at the answer to the next four questions: After the High Court's order, who took the decision not to file an appeal to the Supreme Court and to issue a fresh passport to Mr Lalit Modi? Has the government lodged a fresh protest with the UK government? What steps has the government taken to enforce the Enforcement Directorate's summons to Mr Lalit Modi? Is the government incapable of protecting the life of Mr Lalit Modi in case he returned to India?

The answer given to these four questions will boggle your mind. The answer was:

'As regards queries at Sl No. 4 to 7, no information is available in EAM's Office. However, your application has been transferred to Ministry of Finance, Ministry of Home Affairs and CPV Division, MEA w.r.t. points 4 to 7.'

The guilty mind is there for everyone to see. And both the answers, quoted above, unmistakably point to Ms Swaraj as the author of the answers.

...AND A PARLIAMENT Q&A

Fortunately, the story does not stop there. Mr Arvind Kumar Singh, MP, asked question no. 33 in the Rajya Sabha. It had four parts. The sum and substance was how many passports had been cancelled during the last three years; how many were restored; details of cases where the government had not filed an appeal against the High Court's order; and who took the decision not to file an appeal in the instant case? There was nothing insidious about the question. This was not under RTI, but in Parliament, and the government was obliged to answer the question. The MEA did, speaking through Ms Swaraj, on 24 July 2015. And in furnishing the answer, the MEA has squarely and conclusively implicated Ms Swaraj of wrongdoing.

The MEA's answer candidly admitted that it may cancel a passport 'on request from investigative agencies to that effect'. On not filing an appeal, MEA admitted that 'the appeal against an order of a High Court before the Hon'ble Supreme Court is decided by the CPV Division of the MEA at the instance of the concerned investigative agency and in consultation with the Ministry of Law & Justice.'

It is now conclusively established that it was the CPV (Consular, Passport and Visa) division of the MEA that took the crucial decisions— not to appeal the High Court's order to the Supreme Court and to issue a fresh passport to Mr Lalit Modi. Were the decisions taken at the instance of the investigative agency concerned? I am absolutely certain the answer is 'No'. Was the Ministry of Law & Justice consulted? I suspect the answer is 'Yes'.

THREE MINISTERS IN THE DOCK

So, three ministers have to answer the numerous questions that arise. Ms Sushma Swaraj, who is constitutionally responsible for the decisions of the CPV division; the redoubtable Mr Arun Jaitley on behalf of the Enforcement Directorate which is the investigative agency; and the clueless Mr Sadanand Gowda, the Minister of Law.

No amount of taunts can wish away the fact that the Lalit Modi–Sushma Swaraj story has abuse of authority, nepotism and conflict of interest written all over the pages. Mr Jaitley asked the Opposition, what offence has Ms Swaraj committed? He could take the Prevention of Corruption Act and turn the page to 'criminal misconduct' under Section 13(1)(d)(ii) and (iii).

PM NARENDRA MODI HAS PROMISES TO KEEP

16 August 2015

Prime Minister Narendra Modi addressed the nation from the ramparts of the Red Fort on 15 August. I listened to his speech with rapt attention, trying to understand his Hindi as much as I could, and I read the newspapers the following morning. It is one year since he made the speech (because I am referring to the speech he made on 15 August 2014) and it is appropriate to take stock of the promises that he had made. So, here is a P & A—Promises (P) and Achievements (A):

P. We take a solemn pledge of working for the welfare of the poor, oppressed, dalits, the exploited and the backward people.
A. Between the budget estimates of 2014–15 and the budget estimates of 2015–16, there was a cut of Rs 135,000 crore in allocation to crucial programmes targeted at the poor, including women, children, dalits and the backward. Between the revised estimates of 2014–15 and the budget estimates of 2015–16, there was a reduction of Rs 75,000 crore. Equity suffered a huge blow.

SWACHH BHARAT, JAN DHAN

P. All schools in the country should have toilets, with separate toilets for girls. This target should be finished within one year and on the next 15

August we should be in a position to announce that there is no school in India without separate toilets for boys and girls.

A. Against a target of 4.19 lakh toilets, by the end of May only 1.21 toilets had been built. On 4 August 2015, the Minister of Human Resource Development claimed that 3.64 lakh toilets had been constructed. Only an audit will reveal how many have running water, how many are cleaned every day, and how many are functional and are used every day.

P. I wish to connect the poorest citizens of the country with the facility of bank accounts. An account holder under Pradhan Mantri Jan Dhan Yojana will be guaranteed an insurance of Rs 1 lakh.

A. The UPA government's Financial Inclusion programme was re-named as Jan Dhan Yojana. By March 2014, under the UPA, 24.3 crore accounts had been opened. As of 11 August 2015, an additional 17.29 crore accounts have been opened. Nearly one-half of these accounts (46.91 per cent) have a zero balance and are dormant, and therefore these account holders are, presumably, not eligible for the insurance cover or the overdraft facility of Rs 5,000 that was promised.

NOT DECISIVE, BUT DIVISIVE

P. I appeal to all the people, whether it is the poison of casteism, communalism, regionalism, discrimination on social and economic basis, let us put a moratorium on all such activities for 10 years.

A. If anything, the forces of sectarianism and divisiveness have become bolder and more vocal. Activities such as ghar wapsi, love jihad, ban-this-and-ban-that (books, beef, jeans, channels, websites), attacks on churches, discrimination in housing and jobs, and moral policing have increased in number and spread. None of the perpetrators has been actually punished. In fact, they have been encouraged by the majoritarian streak that runs through the Rashtriya Swayamsevak Sangh (RSS), the BJP and the Modi government.

According to figures of the Ministry of Home Affairs, between January and May 2015, incidents of communal violence had increased by 24 per cent (287 incidents) compared to the same period in 2014 (232 incidents), and deaths in communal incidents had increased from 26 to 43.

P. If we have to promote the development of our country, then our mission has to be 'Skill Development' and 'Skilled India'.
A. The National Skill Development Mission that was launched in 2010 was re-launched on 14 July 2015! Everything else—the STAR scheme, the Skills Councils, the training institutions, the rewards, and the chairman—are the same.

SIGNS OF ECONOMIC STRESS

P. If we have to develop a balance between imports and exports, we will have to strengthen the manufacturing sector. Come, manufacture in India. Sell in any country of the world, but manufacture here.
A. June 2015 marked the seventh straight month of decline in exports, year-on-year. During the seven-month period, exports have shrunk by 14.11 per cent. The Federation of Indian Exporters Organisation has warned that exports may decline significantly even in volume terms which will lead to lay-offs and retrenchments.

There are other indications of economic stress. Year-on-year growth of the core sector was 3 per cent in June 2015 (versus 8.7 per cent in June 2014). Non-food credit growth was 8.4 per cent (versus 13.5 per cent), the slowest in 20 years.

P. Within a short period, we will replace the Planning Commission with a new institution having a new body, a new soul, a new thinking, a new direction, a new faith towards forging a new direction to lead the country.
A. The Planning Commission was abolished. After a long gap, NITI Aayog was established. It has been stripped of the powers enjoyed by the erstwhile Planning Commission, including the power to allocate Plan funds to the state governments and the ministries/departments of the central government. The current five-year Plan will end in 2017, but there is no clarity whether there will be another five-year Plan at all. If

there will be a Plan, it is not clear who will be responsible to make the Plan and who will be responsible for resource allocation.

As I write this on Friday, I look forward to another speech and more promises! Happy Independence Day!

THE OROP WHODUNIT

13 September 2015

The mystery story running on our screens is One Rank One Pension (OROP).

Actually, there is no mystery. All the facts are recorded and documented. However, in the race to claim credit (and disown criticism), the OROP issue is being presented as a big controversy shrouded in mystery.

GET THE FACTS RIGHT

Let's get the facts right. The Indian armed forces are voluntary forces. There is no conscription. Men and women join the forces as jawans or officers for a variety of reasons and, among them, is the security of a job. While the job is reasonably secure, it is not a job for the entire working life. According to the report of the Koshiyari Committee, 85 per cent of the armed forces personnel retire by the age of 38 years and another 10 per cent retire by the age of 46 years. They have to work for a living for many more years, but there is no guarantee of a post-retirement job. Retirement at an early age is good and necessary to keep the forces young and fighting fit. Hence the case for an honourable pension.

There is another reason to make pension an attractive term of service that has not been noticed adequately: it is to attract new volunteers. The attrition rates, and the vacancy levels, are alarmingly high and, if the armed forces are to remain voluntary forces, recruitment must remain robust. The promise of an honourable pension is an important factor in recruitment.

OROP is an honourable pension. The time to debate the merits and demerits of OROP is over. It was a decision taken by the UPA government and reiterated by the NDA government. Both may share credit.

Some more undisputed facts: While presenting the interim budget for 2014–15 on 17 February 2014, I had said: 'During the tenure of the UPA governments, changes in the pension rules applicable to the defence services were notified on three occasions in 2006, 2010 and 2013. As a result, the gap between pre-2006 retirees and post-2006 retirees has been closed in four ranks (subject to some anomalies that are being addressed): Havildar, Naib Subedar, Subedar and Subedar Major... [The] government has therefore decided to walk the last mile and close the gap for all retirees in all ranks. I am happy to announce that the government has accepted the principle of One Rank One Pension for the defence forces.'

WHAT IS OROP?

On 26 February 2014, the Ministry of Defence defined OROP and the following definition was communicated to the chiefs of the three Services: 'OROP implies that uniform pension be paid to the Armed Forces personnel retiring in the same rank with the same length of service irrespective of their date of retirement and any future enhancement in the rates of pension to be automatically passed on to the past pensioners. This implies bridging the gap between the rate of pension of the current pensioners and the past pensioners, and also future enhancements in the rate of pension to be automatically passed on to the past pensioners.'

The four-page, 12-paragraph letter left no doubt on what was intended to be done. The conditions, modalities and the manner of implementation were spelt out in detail. On 22 April 2014 a Working Group was constituted with the Controller General of Defence Accounts as the chairperson with Terms of Reference that included 'to work out the detailed financial implications.' It was specifically stated that 'since substantial increase is anticipated in expenditure on OROP, FA (DS) would thereafter seek additional funds as per requirement.'

Much is made of the fact that the interim budget provided only Rs 500 crore. It was, as I had said, an estimate and the money was provided as 'an earnest of the UPA government's commitment.' Mr Arun Jaitley reaffirmed the commitment in his budget speech on 10 July 2014. And, pray, how much did he provide? He said, 'We propose to set aside a further sum of Rs 1,000 crore to meet this year's requirement'!

So, why is the government adding ifs and buts? Why is the government adding unacceptable riders or conditions that will dilute the 'commitment' of two successive governments?

REJECT THE OBJECTIONS

The sticking points are entirely due to bureaucratic back-pedalling and the inability of the government to overrule the objections. The promise must prevail over the objections, even if some of them appear valid. The promise was to implement OROP from 1 April 2014, and not 1 July 2014. The promise was same pension to personnel retiring in the same rank with the same length of service, and not grant of same pension by looking into the cause of retirement. The promise was that future enhancements in the rate of pension will be automatically passed on to past pensioners, and not that the adjustment will be made every five years.

OROP is a defined benefit pension and different from the National Pension System (NPS) which is a contributory pension scheme. A person who has a short working life in the armed services cannot contribute enough during that period to earn an honourable pension. Hence OROP.

Whatever it takes to implement OROP, the resources must be found. In 2010–11, the Reserve Bank of India (RBI) transferred to the government a surplus of Rs 15,009 crore. Who thought RBI would transfer Rs 65,896 crore in 2015–16? If there is the will, a way can be found.

SEARCHING FOR A METHOD IN THE MADNESS

20 December 2015

It is said 'there is a method in the madness'.

The Bihar election had a lesson for everybody. The BJP learned that there was no one-size Modi cap that will fit all states. The Congress learned that it could not be the lead player—or a lone player—in all situations. The Janata Dal (United) and the Rashtriya Janata Dal learned that there is no such thing as permanent friends or permanent enemies and they have to work hard to remain friends.

One-state parties also learned their lesson in a quiet way. If you are a one-state party, that state is where you belong and that is where you should stay and guard your turf. It is a lesson learned many years ago by the Dravida Munnetra Kazhagam, All India Anna Dravida Munnetra Kazhagam and the Biju Janata Dal and, subsequently, by the Akali Dal and the Shiv Sena. The Samajwadi Party and the Trinamool Congress have now learned that lesson; Aam Aadmi Party will do so soon.

The general expectation, therefore, was there would be sobriety and moderation and all organs of the State would get down to business.

THE GLOBAL SCARE

A quick review of the global situation is necessary to set the context. After the terror attacks in Paris (13 November 2015) and in San Bernardino,

United States (2 December 2015), every country has turned more insecure and, therefore, more inward. Unfortunately, terror is now linked to immigration and anyone with dark skin or a beard or a Muslim name is suspect. Russia, France, then the United Kingdom, and now even Germany have no qualms about going far beyond their borders to strike at the enemies of their countries.

Terrorism now tops the agenda of the advanced—and also, militarily, the most powerful—countries. Mercifully, they spared some time for climate change and will do so for world trade. Once they have sewn up agreements on these two matters, they will go back to their foremost concern—terrorism. Given the scale and reach of the terrorist groups, especially the ISIS, it is difficult to find no merit at all (though there is much to fault) in the approach of the countries that appear to be the most vulnerable to terror.

The world will not notice if India falls off the ladder and that is what we seem to be doing—stumbling as we climb the ladder.

The Parliament session that began on 26 November 2015 offered a great opportunity to rebuild relationships between the government and the Opposition. The Goods and Services Tax issue was a low-hanging fruit. The report of the committee chaired by the Chief Economic Adviser could have been used to pave the way for an agreement on the three contentious issues: the 1 per cent additional tax was anyway dead, no state was totally opposed to a dispute resolution mechanism, and a rate cap could have been provided through skilful drafting.

THE NATIONAL HERALD CASE

A government must always be prepared for the unexpected. On the *National Herald* issue, it appears that the government was prepared for the expected. The government seems to have expected the verdict of the court. Weeks before the verdict, the government seemed to take sides in the private case: it entertained a letter from the private complainant, virtually sacked the Director of the Enforcement Directorate, and reopened an inquiry that had been closed by the former director. So, when the judgement was delivered, the government's and the BJP's spokespersons were ready to fire away at the Congress.

Once the war of words begins, truth is the casualty. The truth in the *National Herald* case is that:

- The income and the assets of Associated Journals Ltd (AJL) remain with AJL;
- The lender to AJL was the Congress party which assigned the loan to a Congress-controlled non-profit company called Young Indian (YI);
- The lender (YI) swapped the loan for equity and became the dominant shareholder in AJL;
- Not a rupee has been taken out of AJL, not a rupee has been received by YI, and not a rupee has been distributed by YI to anyone.

The government, for no reason at all, jumped into the battle and took sides.

MORE FOOLISHNESS

As the *National Herald* issue was again moving toward the courts, the Central Bureau of Investigation (CBI) 'raided' the office of Mr Arvind Kejriwal, the Chief Minister of Delhi. The CBI claimed to be looking for old files relating to the education, health and information technology departments in which a secretary to the Chief Minister had worked some years ago. How did the CBI expect to find those files (old and belonging to other departments) in the Chief Minister's office? No answer. In the end, the CBI did not find those files in Mr Kejriwal's office and only lived up to its reputation of being a 'caged parrot'.

Even as the war of words over the raid on Mr Kejriwal's office was raging, the Governor of Arunachal Pradesh (a BJP government appointee) took the extraordinary step of summoning the legislative assembly, without the customary advice of the state Cabinet, to impeach the Speaker. The unstated goal was to install a BJP government comprising defectors from the Congress party!

'Criminalising' the *National Herald* case, raiding a chief minister's office and using a governor to destabilise the government in a sensitive border state are, in my view, nothing but madness. I wonder if anyone can discover a method in the madness.

ECONOMY

TRUTH, DAMNED TRUTH AND STATISTICS

8 February 2015

Truth hurts. The UPA governments wasted the opportunity that was provided in May 2004 by the outgoing NDA government which had put the Indian economy on the growth path. The last year of the Vajpayee government, 2003–04, was the best ever—not just reckoning the years since 1947 but even going back to the last century, to the years of the East India Company, to the reign of Akbar and of Ashoka, and to the time when our forefathers had discovered Pythagoras's theorem, mastered the art of organ transplant and flew aircraft to other planets.

We must forget the past. Memories are dangerous in a democracy. We must filter memories through the prism of our individual or political preferences to create our perceptions.

FORGET GDP GROWTH

Let us begin by forgetting the GDP numbers between 2004–05 and 2011–12. Let us tell the people that GDP is an imperfect measure, that growth collapsed in 2008–09, that the economy has not yet recovered, and that 'achche din aanewale hain' (good days are coming). Let us tell the people that China achieved the best growth rate during the last 10 years and that means India achieved the worst growth rate. Since India is incomparable, there is no need to bother about the other countries.

Let us forget that Lehman Brothers collapsed in September 2008 triggering what is now called the Great Recession. Bankruptcy is not an uncommon event, so what is the fuss about? Let us tell ourselves that the Great Recession was a period of growth and it was, after all, only the Great Recession and not the Great Depression of the 1930s. Yet the UPA government could record only growth rates of below 5 per cent in 2012–13 and 2013–14. (It has since been revised by a fellow called Anant to 5.1 per cent and 6.9 per cent, respectively.)

COMPARISON OF GDP
Growth rate during UPA-I (%, year-on-year)

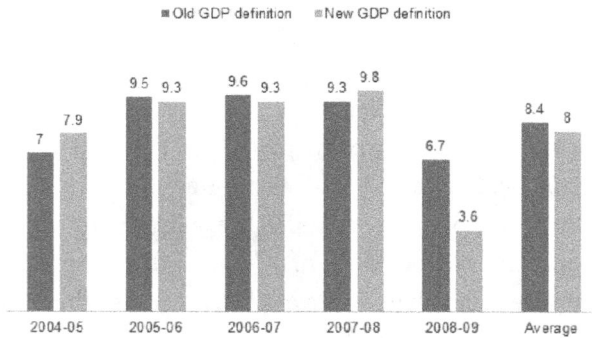

Growth rate during UPA-II (%, year-on-year)

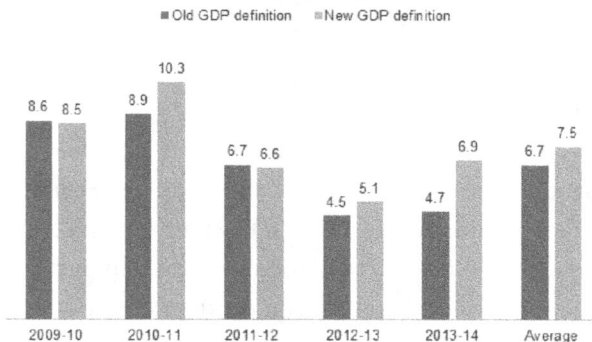

Note: Base year for 2012–13 and 2013–14 is 2011–12 for new numbers and 2004–05 for the old figures. For the rest, the base is 2004–05.
Source: MOSPI

Let us not fool ourselves that a jump in the growth rate from 5.1 per cent to 6.9 per cent was a 'recovery'. Let us also forget that the average rate of growth during the 10 years of UPA was 7.5 per cent (or 7.7 per cent according to that fellow Anant). It was the highest decadal growth since Independence. So what? We achieved higher growth rates during the Vedic period and that was conclusively proved in a paper published at the Indian Science Congress. It will be reaffirmed in a paper that will be presented at the next Indian Mythology Congress. Anyway, 7.5 per cent or 7.7 per cent is still lower than the 7.9 per cent achieved by the NDA government in 2003–04. No matter that the former is the ten-year average and the latter is for only one year. It is easier to trumpet a solitary number than an average because people like an uncomplicated number.

FORGET THE ACHIEVEMENTS

Let us forget the data that shows

- that food grain production increased from 212 million tonnes in 2003–04 to 264 million tonnes in 2013–14;
- that installed capacity of power generation utilities jumped from 112,683 mw in March 2004 to 243,028 mw in March 2014;
- that tele-density rose from 7 per 100 persons in March 2004 to 75 per 100 persons in March 2014;
- that whatever be the starting point, the poverty ratio declined by at least 15 percentage points.

That fellow Anant's data also shows that, during the UPA's tenure, government expenditure as a percentage of GDP actually decreased. Public debt as a proportion of GDP came down from 61.1 per cent in 2003–04 to 49.4 per cent in 2013–14. The current account deficit had been contained at 1.7 per cent of GDP. The fiscal health of the country at the end of March 2014 was good, may be even robust. The share of manufacturing in GDP was 17.3 per cent and not 12.9 per cent as was believed. Mining and manufacturing were wrongly assumed to be contracting in 2013–14, while they actually grew at 5.4 per cent and 5.3 per cent, respectively. 'Make in India' was already underway.

FORGET THE NEW IDEAS

Let us forget that the UPA brought new ideas to the table, such as nutrient-based subsidy for fertilisers, Aadhaar and Direct Benefit Transfer. It drew the blueprint for growth-enhancing reforms such as Goods and Services Tax and Direct Taxes Code. Let us chuckle that it did not draw on its political capital (limited by the lack of an absolute majority) to accelerate their implementation.

These are inconvenient truths and are best left in the recesses of our memory. Ignore the hack who wrote the editorial that said, 'The previous government did a decent job of running the economy but a lousy one of noticing it and letting the public know.'

Let the truth remain shrouded by the froth of corruption charges. Let nothing—certainly not due process—come between 'being called a witch' and 'being burned at the stake'.

Truth be damned. And statistics are lies.

It is time to give marching orders to Anant—following Avinash Chander and Sujatha Singh.

FOURTEENTH FINANCE COMMISSION: GENEROUS TO A FAULT?

1 March 2015

Dissent is the soul of debate. Justice Felix Frankfurter of the United States Supreme Court and Justice K. Subba Rao of the Supreme Court of India wrote many famous dissenting judgements. The most celebrated dissenting judgement in the history of Indian courts was authored by Justice H. R. Khanna in the case of *ADM Jabalpur*. According to Chief Justice Hughes of the US Supreme Court, 'a dissent in the court of last resort is an appeal to the brooding spirit of the law, to the intelligence of a future day when a later decision may possibly correct the error...'

Mr Abhijit Sen can take heart that he may not be alone when he wrote his four-page dissent to the Report of the Fourteenth Finance Commission (FFC). It deserved a more reasoned response than the rather dismissive one-paragraph reply appended by the chairman and the other members of the FFC.

Be that as it may, let us examine the issue objectively.

TRANSFER OF FUNDS TO THE STATES

Should the central government transfer more resources to state governments? My view is yes, a resounding yes. Resource transfers fall under four heads. They are:

1. States' share of taxes and duties (mandatory under Article 270 of the Constitution);
2. Non-Plan grants and loans (discretionary, based on the discretion of line ministries and departments);
3. Central assistance to states' Plans (hitherto based on agreement between the Planning Commission and the state concerned); and
4. Central assistance for central government schemes (discretionary, but governed by principles of burden-sharing).

I have long held the view that states' share of taxes and duties collected by the Centre must be significantly increased. I have also long held the view that central government schemes must be very few and must be fully funded by the Centre. If matters had stopped there, there would be no dispute. The states would have to make do with their share of taxes and duties transferred to them and their own resource mobilization.

Matters did not stop there. The Centre wanted the states to implement its Plan; it also wanted the states to draw up state Plans. The states asked for money, Gross Budgetary Support (GBS) came into being, and the Planning Commission became the arbiter. Besides, just as the Centre had its non-Plan schemes, so did the states have their non-Plan schemes, and wanted money for those schemes too. Article 275 of the Constitution came in handy. Instead of co-operative federalism, the Centre and the states began to quarrel over transfer of funds under Article 275.

UPA SET THE BALL ROLLING

On 2 January 2013, the UPA government constituted the FFC as required under Article 280 of the Constitution. One of the terms of reference was to recommend 'the principles which should govern the grants-in-aid of the revenues of the states.' Further, on 17 February 2014, while presenting the interim budget for 2014–15, I announced that the Centrally Sponsored Schemes (CSS) had been restructured into 66 progammes, and funds for the schemes would be released as central assistance to state Plans.

Consequently, central assistance to state Plans rose dramatically from Rs 136,254 crore in 2013–14 to Rs 338,562 crore in 2014–15.

The UPA government had set the ball rolling. Mr Jaitley maintained the same numbers when he presented the regular budget in July 2014.

The FFC has kicked the ball further. In major shifts from the past, it has increased the states' share of taxes and duties from 32 per cent to 42 per cent. It has recommended grants only for revenue deficit, disaster relief and local bodies. All other grants have been axed. Instead, the FFC has recommended a separate institutional arrangement for grants to sectors such as health, education, drinking water and sanitation. The result: more untied funds to the states. The expectation: more financial responsibility on the part of the states.

SEN'S AGREEMENT AND DISSENT

Mr Abhijit Sen does not disagree with the core recommendations of the FFC. His main concern is that major shifts from past practice will 'disrupt existing Plan transfers with likely very serious effects in the first year of the award period.' He has, therefore, recommended that the states' share of taxes be kept at 38 per cent in the first year and maintained at that level until there is agreement on the separate institutional arrangement. Post agreement, he supports states' share being raised to 42 per cent.

The chairman and other members have responded that it is 'for the authorities to determine the transition path and make arrangements as are appropriate.' The central government, characteristically, has played safe. It has accepted that the states' share of taxes and duties will be 42 per cent but, in respect of grants-in-aid of revenue and revenue deficit grant, it has accepted the recommendations only 'in principle'. The government has also promised to put in place an appropriate institutional arrangement.

All this may seem arcane. Not if you believe that Normal Central Assistance (to the Plan), Rashtriya Krishi Vikas Yojana and Backward Regions Grant Fund, specifically referred to by Mr Sen, are important interventions. Mr Sen has appealed to the 'intelligence of a future day'. That day was yesterday, and when you read this column on Sunday you will know if the government has found a satisfactory solution.

WHO WANTS THE RUPEE AT 40 TO THE DOLLAR?

5 April 2015

Who wants the rupee to trade at Rs 40 to one US dollar?

Not Prime Minister Narendra Modi. Not Ms Sushma Swaraj (who famously tweeted in August 2013, 'The rupee has lost its value. The Prime Minister has lost his grace'). At least not any more, and it would not be polite to remind them of their promise during the election campaign last year. We should be happy that that was a promise the government has not kept.

Mr Arun Jaitley, the Finance Minister, was a model of discretion when he said a few days ago that 'the government would like the rupee to reflect its real value.' He is aware that the rupee has appreciated slightly more than 20 per cent against the euro in the fiscal year 2014–15.

Against six currencies, the trade weighted real effective exchange rate (REER) has risen from 109.58 in February 2014 to 124.34 in February 2015. Change in the REER measures the change in the relative value of the rupee vis-à-vis the chosen basket of currencies. Rarely does any currency trade at its real value on every day of the year. It is normal for a currency to witness bouts of appreciation or depreciation but, over a long period of time, a currency must reflect its real value.

RUPEE VALUE WILL CHANGE

Several factors affect the value of the rupee. The obvious factor is the rate of inflation relative to the rates of inflation in our key trading partner–countries. The second factor is inflows and outflows that will strengthen or weaken the currency. The third factor is productivity changes in India. Monetary policies of the major developed countries will also impact the currency of a developing country like India: recall the 'taper tantrum' (to quote the IMF's Managing Director) of the US Federal Reserve in May 2013.

2014 was an unusual year. Developed economies were crawling with low inflation and low growth, oil prices had collapsed, and commodity prices had declined sharply. India's high interest rates attracted large quantities of foreign funds. The current account deficit remained under control and fiscal consolidation was on track. The value of the rupee was reasonably stable, especially against the dollar, but then came new problems.

The rupee appreciated against other currencies and exports were sharply affected. In February 2015, exports fell by 15 per cent year-on-year. That was the third successive month of decline. There was negative growth, year-on-year, in the export of manufactured goods including leather and leather products, engineering goods and electronic goods.

High interest rates bring their own problems. Export competitiveness of manufacturers and exporters is eroded. Large inflows of foreign funds, especially into the capital markets, will force the Reserve Bank of India (RBI) to buy foreign currencies (especially dollars) to arrest the appreciation of the rupee. If managing the exchange rate takes precedence, managing inflation will take a knock.

THE GATHERING CLOUDS

There are clouds on the horizon. The first is, what will the US Federal Reserve do? Will it hike interest rates?

The second is declining exports. Export earnings are a stable source of foreign exchange. Rising exports also boost manufacturing, increase demand for a variety of services, and create jobs. I am afraid we may have missed the export target for 2014–15 and only barely equalled the export value of goods in 2013–14 (US$ 312 billion). Key export sectors such as textiles, gems and jewellery, and drugs and pharmaceuticals have seen a decline in their share of total exports.

The third worry is the sluggish performance of the core sector. At the end of February 2015, overall growth of the eight sectors is 1.4 per cent as against 6.1 per cent at the end of February 2014. Of the eight sectors, only coal, cement and electricity have registered growth at 11.6, 2.7 and 5.2 per cent respectively. The decline in steel is particularly worrying— from 11.5 per cent at the end of February 2014 to (–)4.4 per cent at the end of February 2015.

Some other pieces of news drifting in should also worry the government. Developments in West Asia and the pressure they may exert on oil prices. Unseasonal rain that has reportedly affected crops on 106 lakh hectares of land. Private flour millers have signed contracts to import 80,000 metric tonnes of Australian wheat.

SHUT OUT DISTRACTIONS

Amidst all these, the value of the rupee should be the least of the concerns, especially when the declared policy is that the exchange rate will be determined by the market. Unfortunately, the election rhetoric and a false sense of pride have clouded the issue. If the exchange rate is a matter of pride, Japan should be only half as proud as India (120 yen to a dollar) and China ten times more (6.2 yuan to a dollar)! My advice is, leave the rupee alone, unless there is unusual or extreme volatility.

The government and the RBI have their work cut out. The Prime Minister should resolutely shut out all distractions (religious conversion, ban on cow slaughter, joint session of Parliament, GUJCOCA, frequent foreign travel) and focus on the economy. Much will depend on reviving export growth, production of coal, generation of electricity, manufacture of steel, cement and fertilisers, accelerating the building of infrastructure especially roads and railways, and enhancing productivity across all activities. There is no time to be lost.

INFLATION IS BAD,
BUT IS DEFLATION GOOD?

26 April 2015

There is satisfaction all around that inflation has declined.

The decline in the rate of inflation began in November 2013 (which was the month when both Consumer Price Index (CPI) inflation and Wholesale Price Index (WPI) inflation had peaked). The decline has been secular, and in November 2014, WPI inflation touched zero. The numbers published in March 2015 estimated WPI inflation at (–)2.33 per cent and CPI inflation at 5.17 per cent.

HAPPY URBAN CONSUMER

None is happier than the consumer, especially the urban consumer. The happiest person is the head of the household because she is the one who buys most goods and services needed by the family. She is still unhappy that prices of some food articles are elevated: the current rate of year-on-year inflation in cereals is 2.32 per cent, milk and milk products is 8.35 per cent, vegetables is 11.26 per cent, fruit is 7.41 per cent, and meat, fish and poultry is 5.11 per cent.

Behind every product or service, there is a producer or service provider. While consumers are generally happy, producers are in distress.

The worst affected are the farmers. Barring a few (who have managed to keep large holdings despite land ceiling laws), most farmers are small landholders and are poor. According to the Situation Assessment Survey of Agricultural Households (December 2013), published by the National Sample Survey Office, 40 per cent of the households of the country are classified as agricultural households. The estimated number is 90.2 million and does not include agricultural labour (that is, landless) households. The survey estimated that 70 per cent of agricultural households own less than one hectare.

The small landowner (owning less than one hectare) will always remain poor—unless he strikes oil or gold on his land. He needs help. He needs to supplement his farm income with non-farm income. He needs help to migrate (or enable his children to migrate) to the non-agricultural sectors. His children need to acquire an education and non-farm skills. Given a choice—and this is very sad—he will give up farming. But the vast majority of farmers do not have that choice. What will they do tomorrow if they give up farming?

UNHAPPY PRODUCER-FARMER

Besides, the rest of the country needs them to continue to do farming and will be horrified if they abandoned farming. Who will produce the 96 million tonnes of wheat, 103 million tonnes of paddy, 18.4 million tonnes of pulses, 355 million tonnes of sugarcane, and 35 million bales of cotton that the country produced in the last agricultural year?

The farm sector is in deep trouble because of a fall in prices. Take a look at the table sourced from the Centre for Monitoring Indian Economy. It contains the monthly average wholesale prices (that is what the producer can expect to get) across various markets in India during March 2014 and March 2015.

	Rs per quintal	
	March 2014	March 2015
Wheat	1,645	1,545
Paddy	1,470	1,445
Sugar	3,249	3,057
Cotton	5,014	4,060
Rubber	14,151	10,723

The decline in prices has left the producer-farmer poorer and deeper in debt. Compounding his woes are unseasonal rain, drought, thunderstorm (in Bihar on 22 April), and the threat of a deficient monsoon as per early forecasts. The government has added to his woes by a paltry increase in Minimum Support Price (MSP), inefficient procurement, increase in prices of fertilisers, poor compensation for lost crop, etc.

This situation did not emerge suddenly. Every government has grappled with these problems. The UPA tried to address them in different ways: introduction of the Mahatma Gandhi National Rural Employment Gurantee Act in 2006 to supplement farm income/wages; farm loan waiver in 2008 to give partial relief from past debt; and generous increases in MSP between 2004 and 2014. The Food Security Act, 2013 was an indirect supplement to income. The Land Acquisition, Rehabilitation and Resettlement Act, 2013, was to give the small landholder an opportunity to exit willingly and migrate to other sectors of the economy. These efforts paid off and agricultural growth during 2009–14 recorded a historic high of 4.06 per cent. Yet much remains to be done, and every successor government is obliged to help the producer-farmers.

DEFLATION AND ITS CONSEQUENCES

The decline in the rate of inflation could be attributed to many reasons. Presently, it is mainly due to the steep fall in the world prices of crude oil and commodities. Lack of adequate demand is another reason. Increase in productivity could lead to an increase in supply and contribute to a decline in prices, but there is no evidence of a sudden rise in productivity in the agricultural or manufacturing sectors. Most commentators agree that there is inadequate demand: indicators of that are low growth rate of bank credit (12.6 per cent in 2014–15), decline in merchandise exports (US$ 310 billion in 2014–15 as against US$ 314 billion in the previous year), and the widely acknowledged fact of absence of new investments.

Consumers need to change their outlook towards producers. Producers must make reasonable profits; if they make losses, they will stop producing. It is profits which sustain production, employment and more investment. Reasonable price increases are the only way to reward producers, especially farmers, and if that means a reasonable level of inflation, consumers must accept it as a necessary concomitant of development.

Deflation is not an unmixed blessing. Sometimes it can be more calamitous than inflation.

HOW LONG CAN HOT AIR KEEP BALLOON AFLOAT?

24 May 2015

In the elections held in 2014, the Congress lost and Mr Narendra Modi won, and I say that advisedly. No one remembers the promises made in the BJP's manifesto or what the party's then tall leaders said. No one remembers what Mr Rajnath Singh, as president of the BJP, said or did or promised—the only memorable episode in which Mr Rajnath Singh featured was when he suggested a billboard with the slogan 'Abki baar, BJP sarkar'. Within minutes the billboard was taken down from the website and the slogan was replaced by 'Abki baar, Modi sarkar'.

The enduring image of that election was Mr Modi, his hologram, his speeches and promises, and his declared position on various issues ranging from Chinese incursions to terrorism to bringing back black money to the value of the rupee. Mr Modi won the election for the BJP and for nearly all the BJP candidates. Wherever he went or spoke, he projected Mr Modi and promised development and jobs. And the ultimate promise was that if you voted for Mr Modi, achche din were round the corner.

DEVELOPMENT AND JOBS

One year later, it is time for a term report.

Mr Modi remains the dominant figure on the political scene. He dominates the BJP, the government, the media space and public discussion. However, he has little impact on Parliament. It is sad that in a parliamentary democracy the prime minister is not the dominant figure in Parliament—but Mr Modi is not the first prime minister to have failed in this regard. He has also made known his dislike for the media by avoiding press conferences or one-on-one interviews. His communication strategy is strictly a one-way street.

That leaves the two important metrics for measuring economic progress: development and jobs.

Hard data come after a lag. Meanwhile, the best way to measure progress on these two metrics is to ask people what, in their view, are the most outstanding achievements of—or what they recall about—the Modi government.

According to a *Times of India*-Ipsos survey (16 May 2015), Swachh Bharat came on top with Jan Dhan and Make in India at a distant second and third. According to Maven Magnet's Conversational Research (*Economic Times*, 17 May 2015), the three top initiatives that elicited a 'favourable' response were Jan Dhan (73 per cent), Make in India (70 per cent) and Swachh Bharat (69 per cent).

Those surveys are a good place to start. For the record, let me say that neither Swachh Bharat nor Jan Dhan figured in Mr Modi's speeches during the election campaign. He did emphasise job creation but did not coin the slogan Make in India until he spoke on 15 August 2014.

Swachh Bharat and Jan Dhan cannot qualify as economic reforms, much less developmental or job-creating initiatives. Swachh Bharat is a social goal or value that must be welcomed, as we did its earlier version, Nirmal Bharat Abhiyan. Jan Dhan is an administrative tool, the same as the No Frills (or Zero Balance) Account, and we welcome the 12 crore new accounts opened under the NDA as we welcomed the 24 crore accounts opened under the UPA until 31 March 2014. Make in India, however, is a clever slogan and a copywriter's dream, and highlights the importance of the manufacturing sector both in development and job creation.

DATA CONTRADICT CLAIMS

Now, let us look at the hard data that would be relevant to 'development' and 'jobs' (see table).

	2013–14	2014–15
Manufacturing*	5.65%	5.38%
Construction*	2.96%	4.6%
Trade, Hotels, Transport, Storage & Communication*	11.52%	8.42%
Financial Services, Real Estate & Business Services*	8.63%	13.71%
Core Sector Growth	4.2%	3.5%
Non–Food Credit Growth	14.2%	8.6%
Merchandise Export Growth	4.91%	1.48%
Number of Private Projects Abandoned/Stalled during the year	444	525

*Year–on–year up to Q3

There are more red lights than green. Yet the GDP is estimated to have grown at 7.4 per cent in 2014–15, although the Reserve Bank of India has warned of a downward revision.

It is not difficult to see what is going right and what is going wrong. When a determined effort was made by the UPA government in 2012–13 to contain inflation and the twin deficits (fiscal and current account), I predicted that the economy will revive in 2013–14. It did, and when the UPA passed on the baton to the NDA in May 2014, the GDP had recorded a growth rate of 6.9 per cent in 2013–14. That momentum and the unexpected bonanza of a collapse of oil prices have carried the NDA government through 2014–15.

THE CAUSES OF WORRY

However, there are worrying signs:

- Investors are in wait-and-see mode, hence credit growth is sluggish;
- Wages and disposable incomes are depressed, hence aggregate demand is low;
- Projects remain shelved or stalled because there is neither a policy nor persistent action on removing the bottlenecks;
- There is no evidence of new manufacturing industries or manufacturing jobs, and that is reflected in the poor performance of the core sector;
- There is no Big idea on bold, structural reforms, the recommendations of the Financial Sector Legislative Reforms Commission are on the backburner, and the Direct Taxes Code has been dumped.

How long can the hot air of rhetoric keep the balloon afloat? The kindest thing that can be said about the Modi government is that it has lost only one year—and, of course, its sheen.

READ GOVERNOR RAJAN: TIME TO WORRY

7 June 2015

On 26 May 2015, our mindspace was occupied by celebrations on the part of the government and criticism on the part of the Opposition. Both were justified. Each one was playing its designated role in a parliamentary democracy. The people of India deserve to hear both sides—even if the faithful don't wish to.

On the last working day of May, the economic data for 2014–15 was out. Growth was up, marginally, from 6.9 per cent in the previous year to 7.3 per cent, with the caution that the growth rate may be revised downwards. There were no surprises in the numbers. The only surprise is that the government still refuses to acknowledge that the economy had stabilised in 2013–14 and cussedly maintains that it inherited a broken economy. Fact is, it did not. Fact also is that nation-building is always unfinished work.

As editors and columnists worked overtime to write their pieces, the Reserve Bank of India (RBI) worked silently and gave its report card three days later. Let me reproduce the exact words of the Monetary Policy Statement: 'Reflecting the balance of risks and the downward revision to GVA estimates for 2014–15, the projection for output growth for 2015–16 has been marked down from 7.8 per cent in April to 7.6 per cent with a downward bias to reflect the uncertainties surrounding these various risks.'

SPLATTERED WITH RED INK

The statement is splattered with red ink. Just consider these words about the agricultural sector: 'Agricultural activity was adversely affected by unseasonal rains and hailstorms in north India during March 2015, impinging on an estimated 9 lakh hectares of area sown under the rabi crop. Reflecting this, the third advance estimates of the Ministry of Agriculture indicate a contraction in foodgrains production by more than 5 per cent in relation to the preceding year's level. Successive estimates have been pointing to a worsening of the situation, with the damage to crops like pulses and oilseeds—where buffer stocks are not available in the central pool—posing an upside risk to food inflation. For the kharif season, the outlook is clouded by the first estimates of the India Meteorological Department (IMD) predicting that the southwest monsoon will be 7 per cent below the long period average. This has been exacerbated by the confirmation of the onset of El Nino by the Australian Bureau of Meteorology.' The IMD has since forecast a deficiency of 12 per cent.

The government is in denial about rural and farmers' distress. When the government thinks and speaks of farmers it is about what a great law it has made to take away the land of the farmers! Mr Nitin Gadkari is reported to have said 'land acquisition is a blessing in disguise for farmers'.

From all parts of the country we hear reports of mounting debt among farmers, denial of fresh crop loans because of unpaid dues, a hike in the interest rate on farm loans to 7 per cent, and rise in prices of fertilisers. The unkindest cut is the paltry increase in minimum support prices—Rs 50 for paddy, wheat and cotton, Rs 10 for sugarcane and Rs nil for soyabean, bajra, maize and groundnut. Meanwhile, in the wholesale markets, prices of commodities such as wheat, paddy, sugar, cotton and rubber have declined, dealing a further blow to producers.

WHERE IS THE SILVER LINING?

Is there a silver lining in industry? Read the RBI: 'The sustained weakness of consumption spending, especially in rural areas... continues to operate as a drag. Corporate sales have contracted. The disappointing earnings performance could have been worse if not for the decline in input costs. Capacity utilization has been falling in several industries, indicative of the slack in the economy. While an upturn in capital goods production seems underway, clear evidence of a revival in investment demand will need to build on the tentative indications of unclogging of stalled investment projects, stabilising of private new investment intentions and improving sales of commercial vehicles. In April, output from core industries constituting 38 per cent of the index of industrial production declined across the board, barring coal production.'

Can we turn to the services sector for succour? Read more from the RBI: 'Leading indicators of services sector activity are emitting mixed signals... The services PMI (Purchasing Managers Index) declined in April 2015, mainly on account of slowdown in new business orders.' There is more bad news: in May 2015, HSBC's PMI slipped under the 50 point mark, indicating contraction.

A CHALLENGE, NOT CRISIS

We can debate, separately, whether the RBI has done its part to facilitate growth. My view is closer to the view of the government. However, the reality is that after cutting the repo rate by 25 basis points, the RBI has, for the present, absolved itself of any further responsibility and has declared its position: 'Monetary easing can only create the enabling conditions for a fuller government policy thrust that hinges around a step up in public investment in several areas that can also crowd in private investment.'

The situation is challenging but not a crisis as we faced in 1991 or 1997 or 2008. The Congress, the United Front and the UPA governments reached outside government to garner ideas and win support. There are solutions, and if the BJP makes the effort it will find that everyone has the welfare of the country at heart.

The messenger has delivered the message. Don't shoot the messenger!

'EXPORT OR PERISH'. HAVE WE CHOSEN 'PERISH'?

5 July 2015

There is a silent crisis brewing on the economic front and the political class seems unconcerned about it.

For the first time in recent years, the total value of exported goods in 2014–15 (US$ 310.45 billion) was less than the corresponding value in 2013–14 (US$ 313.26 billion). It was attributed to a slowdown in the world economy, a tepid recovery in India, and the fact that a new government had yet to find its feet and address the problems. The year ended in March 2015 on a note of disappointment but not gloom.

Since April 2015, the situation seems to have turned for the worse. We have the numbers for the whole of 2014–15 and up to May 2015. A trend is discernible and it is worrying. Year-on-year (y-o-y), exports of goods have declined in every month since December 2014, and May 2015 marked the sixth month of decline in succession (see table).

Month	USD million	Y-O-Y change
December 2014	26,020	−1.41%
January 2015	23,775	−11.58%
February	21,826	−13.88%
March	23,884	−21.29%
April	21,987	−14.76%
May	22,346	−20.18%

NO EXCUSES PLEASE

I can hear the first sounds of the blame game. It will be said, 'It's because of the slump in POL (petroleum, oil and lubricants) exports.' True, the decline in POL exports was a major contributor, but even non-POL exports have recorded a decline for four months in succession (January to April 2015). May 2015, for which figures are not yet available, was not likely to have been different.

It will be said, 'This is a legacy of the UPA government.' Wrong. In 2013–14, export growth was positive at 4.3 per cent. From April to November 2014, growth was positive in every month except October. Total exports of goods in 2014–15 would have been positive but for the downturn that began in December 2014. In fact, it was the performance in the months of December 2014 to March 2015 that caused the year to end on a negative note.

There is, of course, a price effect on the value of exports. If the price of crude oil falls, the value of POL exports will also fall. There is a price effect on the export of gems and jewellery as well. But if prices are more or less the same for certain goods and commodities, a decline in the value of exports of those goods and commodities points to serious problems of demand and competitiveness. Such a decline can be noticed in agriculture & allied products; ores & minerals; leather & leather manufactures; chemicals & related products; engineering goods; electronic goods; and other manufactured goods. Only the readymade garments sector seems to be holding out.

Export of services was relatively better, registering a small positive growth in all but three months of 2014–15. However, there was negative growth in March (–1.89) and April (–4.55), a rare occurrence and, therefore, worrying.

COMPETITIVENESS ERODED

Let us examine what may have gone wrong. An obvious reason is that global demand remained muted. All major economies have slowed down.

Yet it is pertinent to point out that countries such as China, Japan and Korea are still recording positive export growth rates. India is among the few with negative growth of exports.

The second obvious reason is the exchange rate. The rupee has strengthened against all major currencies except the dollar. The central bank's Governor Rajan has spent time 'educating' the BJP leadership that there can be no greater catastrophe than fulfilling the BJP's election promise of upping the value of the rupee to Rs 40 to a US dollar! He has tried to depreciate the rupee but has succeeded so far only in preventing its rapid appreciation. The government takes pride (legitimately) in wooing foreign investments, but the high inflow of capital is putting upward pressure on the rupee. Dr Rajan's interest rate policy is also a contributor to huge capital inflows. Managing the exchange rate, and keeping it competitive for exports, is the most difficult task of the government/ Reserve Bank of India (RBI). Mr Narendra Modi's long stint as chief minister did not prepare him for that.

The fundamental issue is the competitiveness of India's exports. Both the government and the RBI have instruments in their hands that can enhance competitiveness. If one factor erodes competitiveness, another factor must be tweaked to enhance competitiveness. That is the short term answer. The long term solution is to enhance the overall efficiency of the economy. Look back, and you will find that periods of robust export growth corresponded to periods of efficiency gains. We must constantly push the envelope to make road and rail transport more efficient, ports more efficient, communications quicker and more reliable, credit abundant and cheaper, electricity cheaper, labour more productive, and compliance with rules and regulations easier. That can only come through bold and fast-paced reforms that were promised but of which there has been scant evidence in the first year of Mr Modi's government.

FIEO SOUNDS ALARM

The Federation of Indian Exporters Organization has warned that exports may decline significantly even in volume terms which will lead to lay-offs and retrenchments.

All these should have stirred the Ministry of Commerce to action. But the Minister, Ms Nirmala Sitharaman, has been unusually silent (like the Prime Minister in the last three weeks) and largely invisible. Why? Doesn't the government care?

WILL SOMEONE PLEASE READ THE TEA LEAVES?

23 August 2015

The Prime Minister is entitled to choose the place and subject of his speech. But the speech on Independence Day is different. Citizens have a right to expect that the Prime Minister will address issues that are of concern to them. There are other interested listeners as well—foreign governments especially governments of neighbouring countries, global civil society, oppressed people, and those who pioneer change.

At the end of the Prime Minister's 90-minute speech, most people were underwhelmed. The applause was infrequent and listless, sections of the audience began to leave after the first hour, and the criticism was scathing. Given his extraordinary oratorical skills, the Prime Minister has no one to blame except himself.

ISSUES IGNORED

I made a list of issues on which the Prime Minister did not speak: the economy, internal security, national security, neighbours, foreign policy, climate change, discrimination against dalits and minorities, increase in communal incidents, issues of women and children, and natural calamities.

Of all the issues, my foremost concern is the economy. It is possible that the Prime Minister is not well-versed on macro-economic issues. That is why there is a finance minister, a chief economic adviser, a governor of the central bank, a NITI Aayog, and a host of officials dealing with different aspects of the economy. It was obvious that the Prime Minister had not taken their inputs for his I-Day speech. If he had thought that the economy was not a subject that deserved to be dealt with at length, that was a pity. If he had thought that the people of India did not care whether he spoke about the economy or not, he was plainly wrong.

Earlier this week, Moody's, the rating agency, lowered the growth forecast for 2015-16 from 7.5 per cent to 7 per cent. GDP growth, under the new series, was 6.9 per cent in 2013-14 and 7.3 per cent in 2014-15. Given that a recovery was underway, one would have expected that the growth rate would accelerate in 2015-16, the first full year of the Modi government. If Moody's forecast turns out to be correct, it would mean that the growth rate will decline in 2015-16.

SIGNS OF ECONOMIC STRESS

Few will be surprised. The signs of stress have been visible in recent months, yet no one in the government seemed to care or took corrective measures.

Credit growth is a crucial indicator. At 8.4 per cent, non-food credit has recorded the slowest rate of growth in 20 years. Bank chairpersons have confided that many weeks have passed without a major big-ticket proposal for a bank loan. Typically, it is the private sector that should provide the lead in new investments, but the private sector is shying away from new investments because corporate incomes and profits have collapsed in the last 12 months. Total corporate income fell in each of the last three quarters ending December 2014, March 2015 and June 2015. The decline, compared to the corresponding period of the previous year (COPPY) is captured in the following numbers:

Quarter ending

		COPPY
December 2014:	−0.14%	6.67%
March 2015:	−6.00%	8.72%
June 2015:	−4.46%	8.98%

As for corporate profits, the numbers are just as bad. Corporate profits shrank by 32.86 per cent in the quarter ended December 2014 and 15.20 per cent in the quarter ended March 2015, and increased by a minuscule 0.43 per cent in the quarter ended June 2015.

New investment proposals are announced and dropped. During the period July 2014 to June 2015, the number of private sector projects that were announced increased from 1,030 (in the previous 12-month period) to 1,253 but the number of projects dropped also increased from 392 to 478.

Exports have declined, month-on-month, for eight successive months from December 2014 to July 2015.

The government seems to think that negative inflation in the wholesale price index is a sign of economic good health. It is not. It could mean that demand is sluggish. Besides, it depresses prices for the producers, especially the farmers, leading to distress in the agriculture sector.

The only silver lining is the increase in public investment. Thanks to an unprecedented fall in oil prices (Brent at less than US$ 50 and WTI at less than US$ 42), the government has got a windfall. It has wisely stepped up capital expenditure. That seems to be the only trick in the government's bag, but that will hardly be sufficient to boost overall investments and growth.

About jobs, the less said the better. The biggest casualty in the first full year of the Modi government is the stagnation in employment. Speak to any group of young men and women—or to their parents—and you will sense their growing anxiety and fear that not enough jobs are being created in the economy.

DUTY TO SPEAK

Will Prime Minister Modi address these issues? It is unlikely, given his style of communication. He loves one-way communication from a high and distant stage to a large crowd. He avoids speaking in Parliament in the same way that he spoke rarely in the Gujarat state legislature, because that will mean he must engage in debate with the Opposition. He is unwilling to address the media, because that will mean he must answer probing questions.

It is sad that Mr Modi has chosen to be silent on the economy, when the people expect him to speak.

AT LAST, WILL WE HAVE AN ECONOMIC AGENDA?

30 August 2015

I have always welcomed the threat of a crisis. That seems to be the only real trigger for debate and discussion in India.

For the first time in 15 months, the BJP/NDA government has been forced on the back foot by external developments. Not everything, however, has changed: for example, ministers continue to mouth the convenient untruth that the economy was in the doldrums in May 2014. *The Hindu* (25 August 2015) reported that Mr Amit Shah, president of the BJP, had said that the Modi government had, in 15 months, raised the average growth of GDP from 4.5 per cent in the 10 years under UPA to 8.2 per cent! I would ask students of economics to examine that statement and tell their class how many words in that sentence are true.

In the wake of the Monday massacre, the Finance Minister rushed to reassure the markets and the investors that all the key indicators have looked up smartly in the last 15 months. Very true. What he did not say was that we reached a fiscal deficit level of 4.1 per cent at the end of March 2015 after crossing two crucial markers of 4.8 per cent in March 2013 and 4.4 per cent in March 2014. So it is with every other indicator like the current account deficit, inflation, foreign exchange reserves, etc. One performs a journey of a thousand miles by crossing the 800th milestone, the 900th milestone and so on.

UNANTICIPATED EVENTS

Not all external developments will be benign. That is the lesson the government has learned in the last week. The crash in oil prices, the decline in commodity prices, and the lifting of sanctions on Iran, created a sense of 'God is in heaven and all is well with the world'. The unanticipated event was the China crisis and the unusual (for the Chinese government) step of multiple devaluations of the yuan.

Such completely unanticipated events have happened before. In September 2008, Lehman Brothers, a leading financial institution, collapsed, triggering a crisis that reverberated throughout the world. At least four European countries touched the brink of insolvency. India's majestic march with an average growth rate of 8.8 per cent (old series) between 2004-05 and 2007-08 was interrupted; nevertheless, the five-year period of UPA I ended with an average of 8.4 per cent.

Similarly, in May 2013, when the Indian economy was stabilising, Mr Ben Bernanke made a thoughtless and unnecessary remark about 'taper'—gradual withdrawal from the purchase of US Treasury bonds. He was rightly castigated for his 'taper tantrum'.

When the Indian economy paid a price for these external developments—for instance, the rupee depreciated—the BJP was merciless in its criticism. That was understandable. What was not was the extravagant promises made—the rupee will rise to Rs 40 to the US dollar (!) and India's GDP will grow at 10 per cent under a BJP government.

On Monday, 24 August, the Sensex shed 1625 points. In August, the rupee has depreciated by about 3.3 per cent against the US dollar. Such volatility and decline in asset prices are stressful. The government will scramble to do something and, even if it succeeds, success will come at a cost. Contrary to popular belief or desire, in a global economy, the government is no longer the lead player, it is more an umpire. We must therefore adjust our understanding and expectation of what the government can and should do.

THE IMPOSSIBLE TRINITY

Take the case of the exchange rate. It is closely linked to two other key issues: (1) an autonomous monetary policy and (2) free capital flows. No government can manage—or fix—all three. That is why it is called the 'impossible trinity'. If the Reserve Bank of India (RBI) keeps the policy interest rate high (to keep inflation down), foreign money will flow in, but the rupee will appreciate making imports cheaper and exports costlier. If the government and the RBI agree to keep a fixed exchange rate, it would mean choosing between imposing capital controls and giving up autonomy on monetary policy, neither of which would be desirable.

Basically, there are three options:

1. Free capital flows and autonomous monetary policy, but a market-determined exchange rate;
2. A fixed exchange rate and autonomous monetary policy, but strict controls on capital flows;
3. A fixed exchange rate and free capital flows, but no autonomous monetary policy.

Which is the correct option? No one is certain. Even the so-called correct option may not work in all circumstances. For many years, China followed the second option, and fared well, but the rapid growth of China's economy and its scale, size and spread of trade made option 2 obsolete.

The safer option appears to be option 1. The fear is flight of capital. It stems from the fact that governments are prone to adopt foolish policies that will frighten investors: run high deficits, make retrospective tax laws, create an un-level playing field, erect hurdles to doing business, not uphold the sanctity of contracts, not protect intellectual property, litigate endlessly or suspect and investigate every transaction. To shed the fear of flight of capital, we must abandon foolish policies and vow to never repeat the mistakes.

I believe the government has learnt its lessons and is beginning to consult a wider spectrum of economists and investors. Let us hope we will now have a coherent economic agenda from the not-so-new government.

CUT IN REPO RATE: NOW, DO THE HEAVY LIFTING

4 October 2015

As they say, it is 'done and dusted'. The Reserve Bank of India (RBI) finally met the expectations of the government, business and a number of economists and cut the repo rate by 50 basis points. The Governor, Dr Raghuram Rajan, was hailed as a hero. He would have been hailed as a hero even if the RBI had cut the repo rate by 25 basis points or not made a cut at all. There are enough economists who would have supported either decision. Bankers would have anyway supported any decision: the RBI is their regulator!

All this is not to be understood as criticism of RBI's decision. I think it was the right decision, and I immediately welcomed it. I also think that it was long overdue—at least by two to four quarters—and the delay may have cost quite a bit of growth.

To understand the RBI's cautious moves, one must understand Dr Rajan. He is an intellectual powerhouse, a tenured professor at the University of Chicago and the author of several path-breaking books. Independent, orthodox and cautious are the words that best describe him.

FISCAL CONSOLIDATION ON TRACK

Dr Rajan believes that price stability is the main objective of monetary policy. He would know that inflation targeting is not done as much by changing rates as by managing inflation expectations by signalling to the market that the central bank is committed to a certain path. He would also know that small changes in the interest rate usually do not have a significant impact on inflation unless inflation expectations are anchored.

With this background, let us consider how well the RBI has conducted monetary policy in the last 24 months.

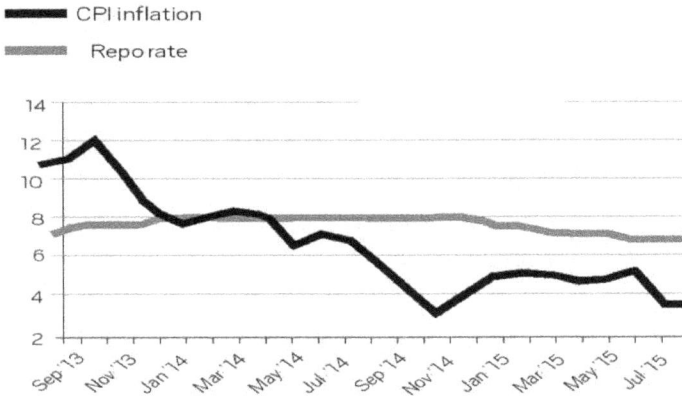

The graph shows year-on-year CPI inflation and the repo rate since September 2013. While reading the graph, please remember that the RBI had, in its monetary policy statements of 2014, set the target of inflation at 8 per cent by January 2015 and 6 per cent by January 2016.

To its credit, the government remained committed to the path of fiscal consolidation announced in 2012, following the report of the Vijay Kelkar committee. The fiscal deficit was to be contained according to the following time table:

March 2013: 5.2 per cent
March 2014: 4.8 per cent
March 2015: 4.2 per cent

March 2016: 3.6 per cent

March 2017: 3.0 per cent

In each year up to March 2015, both under the UPA and NDA, we have done better than the target.

And then came the oil and commodities bonanza. The collapse of prices made the government's job easier. It could expand public expenditure and at the same time achieve the fiscal deficit targets.

FORMULATING MONETARY POLICY

Now, let's read the graph closely. Inflation peaked in November 2013. Since then it has fallen dramatically. Between November 2013 and May 2014 (the UPA period), CPI inflation declined from 12.2 per cent to 8.3 per cent. Between May 2014 and August 2015 (the NDA period), CPI inflation declined from 8.3 per cent to 3.7 per cent. In the process, the RBI's target of 8 per cent by January 2015 was easily achieved and, I am confident, the target of 6 per cent by January 2016 will also be achieved.

Contrast this with the repo rate decisions during the period. Till January 2014, interest rates were increased in small steps of 25 basis points. Through 2014, the repo rate was held unchanged at 8 per cent when there was a steep decline in inflation. However, Dr Rajan did three rate cuts in 2015 when inflation was more or less constant. RBI's actions were contrarian. RBI expected inflation to rise after June 2015; in hindsight, it appears that RBI's inflation forecasts were flawed.

One could argue that if the inflation forecasts had been more accurate, the cuts could have been deeper and sooner. That would have improved liquidity, boosted consumption, and given confidence to investors.

Formulating monetary policy is a complex exercise. It requires making difficult judgments based on limited (and often unreliable) data. The burden is too much on one individual, however exceptionally qualified he or she may be. Hence the need for a Monetary Policy Committee (MPC). I have pleaded for an MPC with equal representation for the government and the RBI and a casting vote for the governor. Despite Dr

Rajan hinting that an agreement has been arrived at, the government has not announced the MPC. Decision-making in the NDA regime remains 'a riddle wrapped in a mystery inside an enigma'.

HEAVY LIFTING AHEAD

The cut in the repo rate is not the end of policy making; it gives the government an opportunity to take bold decisions. Over the next few months, it is the government that must do the heavy lifting: persuade domestic investors to invest; get the promised Foreign Direct Investment; resolve the new tax issues that have cropped up post May 2014; lift the production of coal, steel, oil, natural gas and electricity; quicken the pace of building infrastructure in roads, railways and ports; and pass the Goods and Services Tax Bill and other Bills by reaching out to the Opposition. Above all, it must not allow fanatics and eccentrics to set the agenda and raise irrelevant issues that distract us from the work of development.

THERE IS A MOUNTAIN TO CLIMB

22 November 2015

Parliament has been summoned to meet on 26 November 2015. The state of the economy requires more than a summons to the Members of Parliament. Contrary to what the government's ministers may say in public—and more in line with what some ministers, many officials and practically all business-persons and bankers say in private—the economy is in poor shape. The tell-tale sign is the flat growth rate: 7.3 per cent in 2014-15, 7.0 per cent in Q1 of 2015-16, and the forecast of 7.3 per cent for the whole of 2015-16.

DISAPPOINTING INDICATORS

Let's look at the usual indicators.

Q2 (June to September) 2015 was the third successive quarter in which net sales of all firms shrunk over the same period last year. In Q2 it shrunk 5.3 per cent over Q2 of 2014-15. The manufacturing sector did worse, with net sales shrinking by 12 per cent. For one-fourth of all non-financial firms, operating profits in Q2 were less than interest expenses. Businesses are in the doldrums.

With poor earnings, businesses are not investing. Total proposed investments in private sector projects in the first 8 months of 2015-16 were about 30 per cent less than in the corresponding period of last year. Firms do not seem eager to borrow to invest. Non-food credit in the current financial year is growing at 8.6 per cent, the slowest rate in nearly 20 years. Credit to industry is growing at an even slower rate at 4.9 per cent (which, net of inflation, is the equivalent of zero growth). Credit to medium enterprises actually declined by 6.7 per cent during this period.

In the first half (April to September) of the current financial year, the index of industrial production grew at 3.94 per cent. If we look at manufacturing alone, it was worse, growing at 2.64 per cent. Core sector industries grew at 2.33 per cent in the first half compared to 5.07 per cent in the first half of last year.

The worst performer was exports. At end-September 2015, merchandise exports had declined by 17.7 per cent over last year. October 2015 marked 11 consecutive months of negative growth. Except readymade garments (2.26 per cent), every other group of manufactured goods witnessed a decline in exports. Receipts from export of services declined by 1.4 per cent in the first half compared to the first half of last year. The global slowdown is indeed a major cause, but the rate of decline is worrying because it has happened even as the value of the rupee has depreciated by 6.6 per cent against the dollar.

HOW TRUE ARE THE CLAIMS?

At the Delhi Economic Conclave, the Prime Minister made four claims:

1. GDP growth is up and inflation is down.

    There is no evidence yet of the former. About the latter, while WPI inflation is down, CPI inflation has inched up since July (3.69 per cent) until October (5.0 per cent). Moreover, food inflation has increased from 2.15 per cent at the end of July 2015 to 5.25 per cent at the end of October 2015, and is expected to rise further. Ask a homemaker about the price of pulses or the cost of healthcare, education or travel and you will get a taste of her anger!

2. Foreign investment is up and the current account deficit is down.

   The government is celebrating the increase in Foreign Direct Investment (FDI) from US$ 36 billion in 2013–14 to US$ 44 billion in 2015–16 as well as the 18 per cent increase in the current year. Between 2005 and 2007, FDI had quadrupled from US$ 9 billion to US$ 37 billion. In 2011–12 it was US$ 46.5 billion. FDI inflows have remained range-bound at US$ 36 to US$ 46 billion and there is no perceptible bounce. The current account deficit is low because prices of crude oil and gold are at a historic low.

3. Revenues are up and interest rates are down.

   The government's tax revenues, overall, are expected to fall short of the budget estimates. The 36 per cent increase in indirect tax collections is due to the hike in excise and customs duties. Net of the additional taxes, the increase in collections is only 11.6 per cent, which is normal. Regarding interest rates, the central bank itself has expressed disappointment that the cuts are not being passed on to borrowers. If interest rates are really down to attractive levels, why is credit growth low?

4. The fiscal deficit is down and the rupee is stable.

   If the government is confident of containing the fiscal deficit, it should restore the target date of 2016–17 to achieve a deficit of 3 per cent. The rupee is not exactly 'stable'—it has depreciated against the dollar but has appreciated against the euro and the yen. Besides, there is no particular virtue in a 'stable' rupee; what is needed is an appropriate exchange rate.

NEED VISION AND HUMILITY

Unless there is an international crisis, India's new 'normal' for GDP growth seems to be 7 per cent, and the government is struggling to achieve that. A sedate growth rate will not put more money in people's pockets, it will not create additional jobs (over and above replacements), and it will not throw up additional resources to tackle the age-old problems that plague infrastructure, delivery of education and healthcare, and providing drinking water, sanitation and housing.

In order to break away from the new 'normal', the government must summon the vision and courage to do bold structural reforms (*à la* 1991–92) as well as the grace and humility to engage the Opposition and accommodate their views.

WHAT IS ECONOMIC REFORM, WHAT IS NOT

29 November 2015

Post-Bihar election, there is talk of returning to the development agenda. I would be the happiest person if the energies of the government and Parliament can be channelised into implementing a solid agenda of development. Development has many models. There is a capitalist view of the market economy that lays emphasis on growth, especially growth of GDP. Growth will indeed add to the national output and raise the per capita income but it may—and often does—increase inequalities of income and wealth.

MARKET ECONOMY 2.0

There is a more nuanced approach to embracing a market economy. Growth is necessary but not sufficient to address age-old problems of poverty, deprivation, denial of opportunity and discrimination. Growth-oriented policies must be accompanied by measures that ensure inclusive growth, deliver the minimum needs to all the people, and promote social justice.

There are other models too. Each model lays stress on 'reforms'. Reform what? Reform acquires different meanings depending upon the time and the context. Some even want the government to attempt to reform religious practices, societal norms and human behaviour.

(Lee Kwan Yew of Singapore banned chewing of gum and advised 'if you have to chew on something, chew on a banana'!)

In the context of development, reform means, mainly, economic reforms, efficient delivery of public services, and some changes in human behaviour through laws, advocacy and persuasion.

In my lexicon, true economic reform is one that makes a clean break from the past, replaces the old with the new, and lays out a new model or a new path that will enhance output, efficiency and distributive justice. In that light, I am afraid, most 'measures' advocated by governments do not qualify as reforms. At best, they may add incrementally to the utility or efficiency of the current model or current path, but that is not reform.

REFORMS AFTER 1991

The modern era of economic reforms began in 1991. I wish to list some policy initiatives that qualify as true reforms:

1. The Foreign Trade Policy that was unveiled in a series of steps between July 1991 and March 1992. We made a bonfire of the Red Book and the thousands of pages of gobbledegook that were passed off as export and import policies. We abolished the office of the Chief Controller of Imports and Exports. We declared that exports and imports of goods will be free. Of course, it took a few years to roll out the policy (and there is still work to be done).
2. The abolition of industrial licenses that freed industries from controls on capacity, technology and prices, and promoted competition. (Did you know that once upon a time if a company produced one bicycle more than its licensed capacity it was liable to be prosecuted?!)
3. The movement away from a fixed exchange rate and towards a market determined exchange rate that was started in July 1991. It was quickly followed by the repeal of the Foreign Exchange Regulation Act and the enactment of the Foreign Exchange Management Act, signalling the change from 'control' to 'regulation'.

4. The virtual creation of the Indian capital market. We abolished the office of Controller of Capital Issues and constituted the Securities and Exchange Board of India. The stock market came to life.

5. The repeal of key chapters of the Monopolies and Restrictive Trade Practices Act. This was followed by the enactment of the Competition Act, 2002. We encouraged large size and scale, but put in place a law to prevent anti-competitive agreements and abuse of dominance.

6. The reduction of tax rates—both direct and indirect—started in 1992 but got a bold and decisive push in the budget of February 1997. Personal income tax rates of 10 per cent, 20 per cent and 30 per cent have become irreversible. (Did you know that once upon a time the marginal rate of personal income tax was 97.5 per cent?)

7. The 1997 agreement between the government and the Reserve Bank of India to end ad hoc Treasury Bills and the automatic monetization of the fiscal deficit. The government was obliged to borrow at market rates of interest and hence focus on containing the fiscal deficit.

8. Disinvestment in public sector enterprises that enabled them to discover their true value and introduced a measure of accountability to shareholders. It also paved the way for the government to exit (1999-2004) from businesses it had no business to run.

9. The adoption of the Public Private Partnership model to garner private resources for public projects. It has yielded mixed results but, with some tweaking, it can be more successful.

10. The abolition of State monopoly in telecommunications and the ushering in of the telecom revolution.

11. The Aadhaar-enabled Direct Benefit Transfer that began slowly, gathered pace, stalled, and has now been re-launched. It will drastically change the regime of subsidies and help us deliver only the absolutely necessary subsidies to the absolutely deserving beneficiaries.

LOW-HANGING FRUIT

If the government is serious about economic reforms, it should try and match the above illustrative list. Swachh Bharat is the re-named and scaled-up Nirmal Bharat Abhiyan to build toilets and change human behaviour. Jan Dhan Yojana is the re-named Financial Inclusion intended to provide the poor easy access to banking services. Neither, however, qualifies as true economic reform.

There are several low-hanging 'reform' fruit: Goods and Services Tax Bill, Direct Taxes Code and the recommendations of the Financial Sector Legislative Reforms Commission. Passing those Bills—through negotiation and accommodation—will be true economic reforms.

BUDGET

WHAT WILL THE FM DO WITH 282?

22 February 2015

There is an interesting fact in the recent economic history of India. There have been only six finance ministers since liberalization in 1991.

With one exception, none of them belonged to a government that had an absolute majority in the Lok Sabha. The exception is Mr Arun Jaitley.

282 is a boon. The government enjoys the support of 282 members of the BJP. Adding the allies, it has the support of 336 members. Some months ago, at a book release, I reminded Mr Jaitley that he has no cause for worry about passing the Finance Bill. My worry is what the Finance Minister will do with his worry-relieving majority.

The first clouds appeared on the horizon immediately after the result of the Delhi elections. I counted the remains of the day: urea prices will remain controlled, the number of subsidised LPG cylinders will remain at 12, and the General Anti Avoidance Rules will remain under deferment.

Course correction is difficult and often painful. It requires more than numbers; it requires courage and conviction.

RHETORIC OR REFORM

Mr Narendra Modi and his ministers started by believing their election rhetoric that the Indian economy was in the doldrums. They hold the belief that the key to lifting economic growth is more 'capitalist' reforms. Examples: the ordinance to amend the Land Acquisition, Rehabilitation and Resettlement Act, the constant talk of 'tax terrorism', and the insidious dilution of environmental standards.

It is possible that the government believes that it is on a reformist course and will plough ahead with more public expenditure (fiscal deficit be damned), more tax sops and benign rules of tax collection (revenue deficit be damned), and a liberal import regime for defence equipment and gold (current account deficit be damned). If all of these and more find a place in Mr Jaitley's budget, he will be hailed as a hero and the Confederation of Indian Industry can be expected to publish another unabashed full page political advertisement.

I sincerely wish Mr Jaitley will resist the temptation of being hailed as a hero. Here is my unsolicited advice.

Temper expectations: The economy has been on the mend since 2013–14, when the growth rate jumped from 5.1 per cent in the previous year to 6.9 per cent, but there is still some distance to go. The Central Statistical Office has estimated that growth in 2014–15 will be 7.4 per cent. Accept the estimate and don't aim for a higher growth rate. Given the current situation, a growth rate of between 7 and 8 per cent will be satisfactory and non-inflationary.

Stick to fiscal consolidation: UPA II lost its way when it prolonged the policy of fiscal stimulus. I requested Mr Vijay Kelkar to suggest a path of fiscal consolidation. He did, we adopted it, and it has paid rich dividends. Inflation has moderated, the exchange rate is reasonably stable, and the credit rating is intact. If the Chief Economic Adviser or the Vice Chairman of NITI Aayog demurs, invite Mr Kelkar for a one-week tutorial that will keep the two gentlemen occupied until budget day. The first numbers that analysts will look for is whether the government has achieved the targeted fiscal deficit of 4.1 per cent in the current year and has set a target of 3.6 per cent for 2015–16.

Increase public sector investment, not government expenditure: Public sector enterprises (PSEs) are woefully reluctant to invest. In 2012, we told them 'Use it or Lose it'. We told them that their profits have to be invested, failing which they should give the government more in the form of dividend. The diktat worked. In 2012–13, the capital expenditure of central PSEs was Rs 1,93,737 crore and in 2013–14 it was Rs 2,57,641 crore. Public sector investment stimulates demand for goods and services, creates jobs, and has a 'drag' effect on private sector investment.

On the other hand, government departments are happy to spend. Departments will ask for more money to spend on buildings, travel, seminars, outsourcing studies, and forming monitoring committees. They will propose 'new and better' schemes and promise to name them after BJP icons. Mr Jaitley should firmly reject such requests and give only a little more than what each department actually spent in 2014–15.

Tax sops may be required, but only for enhanced savings: Tax concessions for financial savings are a good idea. Higher deduction under some heads of expenditure is a bad idea. Ideally, exemptions and deductions must go, so that everyone above an income threshold pays tax.

The budget should pass the equity test: On equity, the government's intentions are suspect and its capacity doubtful. Scarce public goods and falling standards impose a huge burden on the poor. There are many ways to promote equity, so let's see how the Finance Minister goes about it.

The budget should also pass the equality test: Rising inequality—of income and wealth—is the bane of development. It is the prime cause of social strife, crime and erosion of democratic values. Only some Scandinavian countries have faced up squarely to this challenge. Given the BJP's core beliefs I can predict, with regret, that the budget will fail the test of reducing inequality.

My best wishes to the Finance Minister!

BUDGET 2015: THE GOOD, THE BAD & THE UGLY

8 March 2015

We may have multiple parties in India but among the 'commentariat' (columnists, letter-writers, tweeters, bloggers and abusers) there are only two benches: the Treasury who can see nothing but good and the Opposition who can see nothing but bad.

I am an honorary member of both. I am also the selector who will unhesitatingly axe that which is plain ugly.

I thought I may share with you some excerpts from Part A of the Finance Minister's budget speech (what he said and what he left unsaid) and my views thereon:

1. 'The credibility of the Indian economy has been re-established': Our efforts since August 2012 have paid off. Recovery began in 2013–14 (6.9 per cent) and continued in 2014–15 (estimate 7.4 per cent) thanks to fiscal consolidation, containing the current account deficit and moderating inflation. **Good.**

2. 'We will move to amend the RBI Act this year, to provide for a Monetary Policy Committee': At last, one major recommendation of the Financial Sector Legislative Reforms Commission will be implemented. Will there be a representative of the government on the committee? Will the governor have a veto? Not revealed. Nonetheless, **Good.**

3. 'I will complete the journey to a fiscal deficit of 3 per cent in three years rather than the two years envisaged previously': If, as claimed, the economy is poised to grow at between 8 per cent and 8.5 per cent, and oil and commodity prices are low, there was no justification to set back the target by one year. *Bad.*

4. 'Our commitment to farmers runs deep': The Rashtriya Krishi Vikas Yojana (RKVY), among other interventions, is credited with pushing agricultural growth to an average rate of 4.06 per cent during 2009–14. Allocation to RKVY has been slashed from Rs 8,449 crore in 2014–15 (RE) to Rs 4,500 crore in 2015–16. Who will fund the gap? Mr Abhijit Sen's warning has gone unheeded. *Bad.*

5. 'Our government is committed to supporting employment through MGNREGA': Under assistance for state Plans, the RE for 2014–15 is Rs 32,456 crore and the BE for 2015–16 is Rs 33,700 crore. There are bills for unpaid wages and hence the net amount available next year will be smaller. Besides, wage rates have gone up and hence the average number of days of employment will come down sharply. Prepare for the slow death of MGNREGA. *Bad.*

6. 'We will bring a comprehensive Bankruptcy Code in fiscal 2015–16': *Good.*

7. 'I, therefore, propose to create a Micro Units Development Refinance Agency (MUDRA) Bank, with a corpus of Rs 20,000 crore, and credit guarantee corpus of Rs 3,000 crore': The government will find the money and then fund the bank, so be patient. *Good (intention only).*

8. 'The soon-to-be-launched Pradhan Mantri Suraksha Bima Yojana will cover accidental death risk of Rs 2 lakh for a premium of just Rs 12 per year. The third Social Security Scheme that I wish to announce is the Pradhan Mantri Jeevan Jyoti Bima Yojana which covers both natural and accidental death risk of Rs 2 lakh. The premium will be Rs 300 per year': Don't make the mistake of assuming these are universal schemes funded by the government. These are standard schemes, depending on voluntary enrolment and annual renewal. It is a promise, it will limp along, and be forgotten after a few years. *Neither Good nor Bad.*

9. 'My government also remains committed to the ongoing welfare schemes for the SCs, STs and women': The numbers tell the sad tale. BE 2014–15, RE 2014–15 and BE 2015–16 for two major disadvantaged groups are as follows: Scheduled Castes Sub Plan—Rs 50,548, Rs 33,638 and Rs 30,851. Tribal Sub Plan—Rs 32,386, Rs 20,535 and Rs 19,980. The actual expenditure in 2014–15 was slashed by one-third, and the allocations have been further reduced for 2015–16. Factoring inflation, the cuts are brutal. For all MPs with a heart and a conscience, especially for those elected from reserved constituencies, it is a call to arms. *Ugly.*

10. 'I intend to establish a National Investment and Infrastructure Fund (NIIF) and find monies to ensure an annual inflow of Rs 20,000 crore to it': We already have the India Infrastructure Finance Company Ltd (IIFCL). We also have the National Investment Fund into which go the proceeds of disinvestment. There is no harm in having one more instrument, provided the government finds the money every year. *Good (but why?).*

11. 'Ports in public sector will be encouraged to corporatise and become companies under the Companies Act': *Good.*

12. 'I hope to garner some additional resources during the year from tax buoyancy. If I am successful, then over and above the budgetary allocation, I will endeavour to enhance allocations to....': That is a pie in the sky. Let the government ensure that revenues do not fall short of the budget estimates before it dreams of additional resources. Nothing can change the fact that the National Rural Employment Guarantee programme, Integrated Child Development Scheme and Integrated Child Protection Scheme have been short changed. *Ugly.*

13. 'I propose to merge the Forward Markets Commission with SEBI': *Good.*

14. 'We will soon be launching a National Skills Mission': There is already a National Skill Development Agency that is in mission mode and spearheading skills development through the 31 Sector Skill Councils. It is duplication, if not duplicity. *Ugly.*

15. 'GIFT in Gujarat was envisaged as an International Finance Centre.

The first phase of GIFT will soon become a reality': Wake up Mumbai! Mr Fadnavis may lose his job if he opposes the idea, but can he survive if he supports it? **Bad, could become Ugly.**

Dear Reader, you can make your own scorecard.

EQUITY SUFFERS A RS 75,000-CRORE BLOW

22 March 2015

The Finance Minister listed 13 points for his Vision 2022. Among them were a roof for each family, clean drinking water, providing medical services, upgrading schools, and increase in agricultural productivity. Everyone agreed wholeheartedly.

He also listed five major challenges but promised that 'the government has decided to continue supporting important national priorities such as agriculture, education, health, MGNREGA, and rural infrastructure including roads. Programmes targeted for the poor and the under-privileged will be continued.' We were reassured.

He cautioned that there would be 'reduced fiscal space for the Centre'. Several commentators, including Dr Y.V. Reddy, Chairman of the Fourteenth Finance Commission (FFC), politely corrected the Finance Minister. The total transfer to the states will be about 62 per cent—which is the same as the average of the past several years and, hence, the fiscal space of the central government will be the same. The change is in the 'untied' and 'tied' proportions. Thanks to the FFC, the 'untied' proportion of funds transferred to the states will increase from 32 per cent to 42 per cent.

The Finance Minister argued that the devolution of a 42 per cent share of taxes is 'an unprecedented increase which would empower states with more resources', and deftly kicked the ball of 'welfare' into the states' corner! I wish to examine his argument in this column.

LESS MONEY, NOT MORE

According to the budget documents, 23 schemes will be fully supported by the central government; 13 schemes will be run on a changed sharing pattern; and 12 schemes will be delinked from the Centre's support. Among the delinked schemes are Normal Central Assistance, Special Central Assistance and Special Plan Assistance—three tools used by the erstwhile Planning Commission to address concerns of regional disparity and inequity.

	Budget 2014–15	Revised 2014–15	Budget 2015–16	BE Difference	RE Difference
CENTRAL ASSISTANCE TO STATE PLAN	314,814	255,874	180,293	134,521	75,581
Rashtriya Krishi Vikas Yojana (RKVY)	9,954	8,444	4,500	5,454	3,944
National Rural Drinking Water Programme	10,891	9,191	2,500	8,391	6,691
ACA for LWE affected districts	2,640	1,760	0	2,640	1,760
Backward Regions Grant Fund–State Component	5,050	3,450	0	5,050	3,450
Normal Central Assistance	28,514	26,814	0	28,514	26,814
Special Central Assistance	11,000	10,150	0	11,000	10,150
Special Plan Assistance	6,837	7,666	0	6,837	7,666

Contd...

National Programme of Mid Day Meals in Schools	4,318	3,997	1,325	2,993	2,672
Sarva Shiksha Abhiyan	9,194	8,894	2,000	7,194	6,894
Backward Regions Grant Fund	5,900	2,837	0	5,900	2,837
Accelerated Irrigation Benefit and Flood Management Programme	8,992	3,277	1,000	7,992	2,277
Integrated Child Development Service	17,858	16,316	8,000	9,858	8,316
Housing for all (Rural)—Indira Awaas Yojana	15,976	10,990	10,000	5,976	990
National Health Mission	21,650	17,434	18,000	3,650	−566
				All figures in Rs crore	

The accompanying table speaks for itself. As against the promised central assistance in 2014–15 of Rs 3,14,814 crore, the government will actually transfer only Rs 2,55,874 crore—a significant reduction of Rs 58,940 crore. And, for 2015–16, there will be a further reduction of Rs 75,581 crore. Now, move down the table. I have picked 14 heads of devolution of funds that support programmes that have contributed to the reduction of poverty and the enhancement of welfare. Under 13 of the 14 heads (the National Health Mission being the exception), the central government will give the states less money next fiscal than what will be spent in 2014–15. Even in the case of NHM, the 'increase' of Rs 566 crore is an optical illusion because it had already suffered a cut of Rs 4,216 crore in the revised estimate of 2014–15.

The government has argued that the shortfall will be more than made up by the increase in the states' share of taxes collected by the central government. According to the budget documents, the Centre will devolve upon the states Rs 5,23,958 crore in 2015–16 as against Rs 3,37,808 crore in 2014–15. But there is a catch: this will happen if the central government collects Rs 14,49,490 crore or about 16 per cent more of tax revenue than what was collected in 2014–15. Assume, reasonably, that the Centre will collect about 13 per cent more in taxes, which was the average percentage during 2009–10 to 2014–15 (and not 16 per cent). That will mean that states' share will be only about Rs 5,09,065 crore. If we assume, uncharitably, that tax revenues will grow at a rate lower than 13 per cent, as it happened in 2013–14 and 2014–15, the share will be even lower.

ABSENT AN ARRANGEMENT

What has budget 2015–16 done? It has reduced the guaranteed component (Central Assistance to State Plan) by Rs 75,000 crore and it may not be able to give the promised increase under the uncertain component (tax share). So, where are the additional resources that the states are presumed to have to fund crucial welfare programmes? Besides, in the absence of an institutional arrangement strongly recommended by the FFC, what is the guarantee that the states will use their 'untied' resources to fund the gap in these programmes? Equity has suffered a cruel blow.

MANY A SLIP BETWEEN THE CUP AND THE LIP

21 June 2015

Making a budget is a task that can be completed with diligence and patience. Making promises—as well as declining to do so—in a budget speech can be done with a mixture of tact and firmness. Allocating money for the promises that demand only small amounts is relatively easy because it will not strain the fiscal deficit. It is keeping the promises made in the budget speech that is the most difficult task of a finance minister.

What looked eminently do-able when the budget speech was written suddenly faces insurmountable hurdles. The minister (of the department) who insisted on the allocation discovers that his department is totally unprepared. The finance minister is perplexed if the money is not spent. The prime minister is upset that his ministers have let him down. The budget division's mandarins chuckle quietly among themselves but wear a grave demeanour at a review meeting. It is only the Department of Expenditure that is genuinely happy that it has saved money for the government! This is a story that has been told many times before.

LEARNING ON THE JOB

Every finance minister (including this writer) is allowed one budget to make mistakes and learn on the job. Mr Arun Jaitley got his chance in the budget for 2014–15.

Counting the mis-hits is a fun sport. The trick is not to lose one's cool (especially the finance minister's) when the mis(takes)-hits are pointed out and counted!

How did Mr Jaitley score in his first budget? Here is a quick count (subject to errors and omissions).

ANNOUNCE AND FORGET

Let me begin with the ones that can be characterised as 'Announce and Forget' schemes. They are one-day wonders that nobody will care to ask about after a few weeks and certainly not after the year is over and it is time for the next budget! Examples:

1. A war memorial was announced, Rs 100 crore was allocated, but it is yet to receive Cabinet approval.
2. A Technology Development Fund to support R&D in defence systems was announced, Rs 100 crore was provided, nothing was spent, and the allocation lapsed.
3. The budget provided Rs 50 crore for a National Police Memorial, RE was Rs 50 crore, which means the sum was spent, on what we do not know, but where is the memorial?

NEVER SAY DIE

There is another set of announcements that can be labelled 'Never Say Die'. A scheme is announced, money is provided, not much—in some cases nothing—is done during the year, but the department won't give up, so money is allocated reluctantly in the next year too, but in some cases for a toned down scheme (see table). Some of them will be 'rationalised' or given a quiet burial in due course!

Scheme/Programme	2014–15 BE	2014–15 RE	2015–16 BE
1. Start Up Village Entrepreneurship	100	1.00	200
2. School Assessment	30	4.20	50
3. New IITs and IIMs	450	15.00	1000
4. Agri-Tech Infrastructure Fund	90	0.10	90
5. National Adaptation Fund for Climate Change	113	10.19	160
6. Price Stabilisation Fund	450	50.00	400
7. National Industrial Corridor Authority	100	7.60	45
8. Technology Centre Network	200	10.00	200
9. Pashmina Wool Development	30	1.00	30
10. Ultra Modern Super Critical Thermal Power Technology	100	13.23	50
11. Upgrading Indoor and Outdoor Stadiums in J&K	200	0.10	100
12. Sports University in Manipur	100	0.10	50
13. Young Leaders Programme	100	12.21	100
14. National Centre for Himalayan Studies	89.40	Nil	100
15. Development of Railway System in Border Areas	1000	Nil	500
16. Setting Up Five Mega Clusters	190	33	100

Rupees in crore

BIG TICKET ITEMS

That brings me to the last set of announcements. These are the big ticket items that are the pride of the budget. Let's see how they fared in 2014–15:

Mr Jaitley's speech gave top billing to the Pradhan Mantri Krishi Sinchayee Yojana. He announced Rs 1,000 crore for the programme. According to the 2015–16 budget papers, only Rs 30 crore was spent. The budget for 2015–16 has allocated Rs 1,800 crore.

There is no bigger icon for the BJP than Mr Deen Dayal Upadhyaya. The government announced the Gram Jyoti Yojana for feeder separation in his name, allocated Rs 500 crore and claims to have spent the whole amount. What is surprising is that nothing has been allocated in the current year. What does that mean? Has the feeder separation been completed all over the country?

Smart Cities was another big idea. For that, and for the Jawaharlal Nehru National Urban Renewal Mission, the allocation was Rs 7,016 crore. However, only Rs 924 crore was spent in 2014–15. The budget papers for 2015–16 show that the old head will get only Rs 143 crore this year and two new heads have been created with an allocation of Rs 5,939 crore.

I do not claim that all budgets in the past were models of transparency. Nevertheless I say that the NDA, which came to power on the plank of greater transparency and effective implementation, has a considerable distance to travel to fulfil its promises.

POLICIES AND PROGRAMMES

JAN DHAN STANDS TALL ON UPA'S SHOULDERS

1 February 2015

Jan Dhan. The name has a nice ring to it. Like two drumbeats. Like the Republic Day march: left-right, jan-dhan, left-right...The purpose of this essay is to recall history. And to ask, how should we move?

One of the grievances against banks, and one of the stated grounds for nationalization of banks in 1969, was that they did not serve the poor. The answer was 'financial inclusion'. Many understood what it meant, few could comprehend the enormous challenge it posed.

Not much was done towards financial inclusion for a long time after 1969, except that banks were directed to open more branches in rural areas. Banks found it was quite profitable to open branches in small towns and large villages. Customers were willing to deposit their money, happy to make small withdrawals, and demanded no other service. Banking meant a pass book and withdrawal slips. It was easy banking, even lazy banking.

FINANCIAL INCLUSION BEGINS

In 2005, the government and the Reserve Bank of India (RBI) directed the banks to open 'no frills accounts'. Since the accounts were allowed even with zero balance, they were also known as 'zero balance accounts'. Soon, this programme too became target-driven. Banks chased numbers.

The RBI took stock and, in 2010, it asked the banks to prepare and implement a financial inclusion plan from 2010 to 2013. In 2012, the 'no frills accounts' got a truly sarkari name—the Basic Savings Bank Deposit Account. In 2013, banks were directed to extend the financial inclusion plan to 2016.

The results—rather, the numbers—were impressive. At the end of March 2014, the number of basic accounts that had been opened stood at 24.3 crore. Blink again. 24.3 crore. There were no boasts, no advertisements.

The biggest challenge was dormancy. Most zero balance accounts had a zero balance and no activity whatsoever.

The first customers to take advantage of this achievement were the women's self-help groups (SHG). They demanded credit from banks, and got credit because of the thrust given to the SHG movement and because women were non-defaulting customers.

However, the big step forward was when the UPA government launched the Direct Benefit Transfer (DBT) scheme. The government directed that all persons who had enrolled for work under the Mahatma Gandhi National Rural Employment Guarantee Act must have a bank account (or a post office account) and that the wages must be credited to those accounts. Millions of bank accounts that had been lying dormant sprung to activity.

The next important step was the government's decision to make cash transfers under 28 schemes to these accounts. The low-hanging fruit were scholarships, pensions, payments to Accredited Social Health Activists and the like.

AADHAAR-ENABLED TRANSFERS

Alongside financial inclusion, the UPA government had launched Aadhaar, the Unique Identity Number programme. We realised that if the bank account was seeded with the Aadhaar of the account holder, it would open the door for better and more efficient management of the numerous subsidy schemes that were plagued by duplication, falsification and leakages.

Practically everyone receives a subsidy—for the LPG cylinder, food, sugar, kerosene, fertilisers and so on. Against opposition, the UPA government decided to transfer the LPG subsidy to Aadhaar-seeded bank accounts. It was rolled out quite smoothly in 121 districts and then extended to 291 districts, but it ran into opposition instigated by those who had profited under the old system. The government buckled under pressure, put the transfers on hold, and appointed a committee (what else!?) to review the scheme. Thankfully, the committee endorsed the Aadhaar-based transfer of the LPG subsidy, paving the way for a re-launch in November 2014.

Despite the BJP rubbishing Aadhaar and DBT while in the Opposition, the NDA government has enthusiastically adopted both. I welcome the intent to roll out the scheme across the country and include as many cash transfers as possible. That is the way to go.

Since 28 August 2014, when the Jan Dhan Yojana was announced, the banks have added 12.14 crore accounts. They stand on top of the 24.3 crore accounts opened earlier. The weakness is that about 75 per cent of the accounts, both old and new, are dormant. There are no transactions in these accounts. It costs the banks Rs 100 per year to maintain each account. That cost eats into the profits of the banks.

Low use of accounts is not an indicator of low demand; it is an indicator of poor service and of products which the customer finds are not useful to her. More cash transfers will stimulate activity, but that activity must be more than mere cash deposits and withdrawals.

The way forward is to use these accounts to channel more than cash. The bank account must be made the prime channel for providing a range of financial services such as insurance, pensions, investments, remittances, tax-related services and, of course, credit. Today, the RBI and the government mandate the banks to 'do this and do that' to promote the goals of financial inclusion. A better way is competition. Allow more banks of all kinds. Regulate the banks, but don't restrict the number or kind. Competition and innovation will drive financial inclusion, not restrictions and mandates.

Good luck to Jan Dhan and its authors. Just remember the pioneers.

NATURAL RESOURCES:
THE FOG IS YET TO CLEAR

29 March 2015

Auctions are the flavour of the season

We were told that auction was the only correct way to transfer the right to use a natural resource. Thankfully, the Supreme Court retracted from that obviously wrong position and approved of any fair, transparent and non-discriminatory method of allocating natural resources.

The numbers have cast a spell. Rs 1,09,000 crore from the auction of spectrum. Rs 2,05,000 crore from the auction of coal mines and growing with every mine put on the block. In the case of spectrum, it is revenue, at no cost, for the central government from an inexhaustible resource. In the case of coal, state governments have been told to expect a windfall over a period of 30 years.

The question that has been asked—and not yet answered by the government—is who will provide these humungous sums of money to the central and state governments. The impression that has been given is that the winners at the auctions will cough up the money. Absolutely untrue.

PAY THROUGH PRICE INCREASE

Where will the money come from?

The first stop will be the banks. The winners will go to the banks, flaunt the allocation orders and ask for loans. The banks will ask them how they propose to repay the loans. The winners will provide a statement of expected revenues. The key factor in the statement will be the 'price' of the final product: electricity, iron and steel, cement, aluminium, etc.

In the regulated sector, such as electricity, the cost of coal is a pass through. The winners will go to the regulator and demand a revised tariff that reflects the increased cost of coal. In some cases, thanks to the reverse bidding method, the winners have bid a negative amount per tonne of coal. In such cases, the pass through will be zero—that is, the cost price of coal will be assumed to be zero! Inevitably, other variable costs will be inflated or the cost of coal will be loaded on the capacity charges and recovered from the distribution company (discom). In turn, the discom will apply to the regulator for an increase in tariff of the electricity that will be sold to the consumers.

In the non-regulated sectors (iron and steel, cement, aluminium, etc.), the cost of coal will be reflected in the 'price' of the final product that will be paid by the consumers.

In the case of spectrum, the cost of acquiring spectrum will be amortised over a period equal to or less than the licence period and the amount of depreciation written in the books of account will be recovered through a revision in the tariff. The revised tariff will be the 'price' at which calls from your mobile will be charged.

REFORM, YES, BUT NOT ENOUGH

The government has claimed that auctioning the resources is a reform. I agree. It is a reform that has put in place a method superior to the first-come-first-serve method adopted in the case of spectrum since 2001 by successive governments. In the case of coal mines, it is a reform that is superior to the method of discretionary allotment followed since 1957 by successive governments. But it is a reform of methodology that does not go far enough.

Some interesting alternatives have been put forward and they deserve to be examined. Mr T.K. Arun has suggested that spectrum could be used as a common pool by telecom service providers on pay-per-use basis. Others have argued that once the government decided to end its monopoly on coal mining, it should have also ended captive mining and allowed the entry of professional mining companies. Alternatively, the government could procure mining services from professional mining companies, mine the coal and run a market for the coal.

BRACE FOR PRICE HIKES

Outright auction of a natural resource like spectrum or coal is easy and it is also an easy way to raise resources for governments. However, it has negative consequences for the consumer as well as the economy. There are anecdotal stories of irrational bidding by companies, especially prior allottees, to retain old or win new coal mines (cases of negative bids). In the case of spectrum, there have been irrational bids by service providers to retain key territories and to protect capital investments already made. Irrational bids will lead to inevitable outcomes: price (or tariff) increase, failing which defaults; lower capital expenditure; and slower roll outs.

In the ultimate analysis, auction is nothing but a transfer of resources from the users of goods and services (consumers) to the owners of the resources (governments). The bills for Rs 1,09,000 crore and Rs 2,05,000 crore will be paid by the consumers. So brace yourself for price increases in many goods and services.

Milan Kundera wrote: 'Man proceeds in the fog. In the fog, he is free, but it is the freedom of a person in a fog: he sees 50 yards ahead, and can observe what is happening close by and react. But when he looks back to judge people of the past, he sees no fog on their path. Looking back, he sees the path, he sees the people proceeding, he sees their mistakes, but not the fog.'

In the allocation of natural resources, the fog is yet to clear.

MONETARY POLICY COMMITTEE: VOTE OR VETO?

2 August 2015

So much has happened that is cause for grief, concern or plain disgust. The universally admired Dr A.P.J. Abdul Kalam passed away. There was a terror attack in Gurdaspur. Amidst a debate on the legality and morality of the death penalty, Yakub Memon was hanged. Cases of molestation or rape continue to be reported every day. The government is unwilling to yield to break the logjam in Parliament.

This week, I would like to draw attention to an issue that is of paramount importance to the economy.

The issue is, 'who will decide the monetary policy?' For the average person, the question can be rephrased to read 'who should decide the policy that will determine the rates of interest at which commercial banks will lend money?' The average person will be right if he assumes it is the government's job, but within the concept of 'government' there are many authorities that are empowered by law to function autonomously and not as an arm of the executive government.

BALANCING GROWTH & INFLATION

The Reserve Bank of India (RBI) is one such authority. RBI is no ordinary bank. It is the central bank, the issuer of currency and bonds, the regulator of commercial banks and non-banking financial institutions, and has other functions as well. In modern economies, it is the central bank that decides the monetary policy. The unstated premise is that the central bank will consult the government. The optimistic belief is that the government will (or should) always agree with the central bank. Alas, that is not true!

The government is concerned with growth, investment and jobs—and also inflation. Only a foolish government will believe that it can ignore inflation as long as there is growth and jobs for the people. A wise government will look for a 'balance': in a developing country the balance is usually expressed in the phrase 'high growth with moderate inflation'.

The central bank's main concern is price stability. In developed countries and in some developing countries, the central bank has just one target—inflation. Many central bankers believe that the central bank must target inflation and only inflation. All recent RBI governors held that view. It appears that Dr Raghuram Rajan also holds the same view, although I can recall conversations with him that led me to think that he did not rule out seeking a balance between promoting growth and targeting inflation.

NOT AT LOGGERHEADS

There is a popular view among commentators that finance ministers and central bank governors are always at loggerheads. That view may make interesting copy, but it is far from the truth. On eight out of 10 monetary policy statements or actions, the government and the RBI will be—and in the past, have been—on the same page. There will, of course, be the occasional disagreement, but that disagreement stems from different assessments of the economic situation at any given time. For example, the government has assessed the current economic situation as non-inflationary and therefore desires a cut in the policy interest rate to stimulate growth. On the contrary, the RBI has assessed the situation as still high on inflationary expectations and therefore wishes to maintain the policy interest rate. No one can be sure who is right. There appears to be an honest disagreement between the government and the RBI.

We need a mechanism that will reconcile the perceptions of the government and the central bank and take an objective view. The Financial Sector Legislative Reforms Commission (FSLRC) has proposed a mechanism: a Monetary Policy Committee (MPC) along the lines obtaining in many countries.

RIVAL PROPOSALS ON MPC

No one seems to be opposed in principle to the MPC or the qualifications and independence required of its members. Differences have emerged regarding the composition and authority of the MPC. FSLRC has advocated a seven-member MPC with three members of the RBI and four external members nominated by the government. The RBI (Urjit Patel Committee report) has recommended a five-member MPC with three members of the RBI and two external members chosen by the RBI. Decisions on monetary policy will be taken by a vote in the MPC. In both proposals, a vote is envisaged, but not a veto to the governor.

I wonder who brought up the question of a veto to the governor. A veto is the antithesis of a vote. A vote and a veto co-exist uneasily and with unhappy consequences only in the UN Security Council!

My view, though unconventional, is there may be a six-member committee—three from the RBI and three external members nominated by the government. In the case of a tie, let the governor have a casting vote. The minutes must be made public. Assuming the three internal members vote alike, the governor needs to persuade at least one external member to agree with him, and on most occasions he will. In situations where all three external members disagree with the three internal members, it will be a brave governor who will vote, every time, in his own favour to break the tie.

I reject the argument that the government cannot be trusted to nominate qualified or independent members. Governor Rajan was appointed by the UPA government and we are proud of the choice. So, let's have a six-member MPC and give the governor a casting vote, but put the onus squarely upon him.

ENCRYPTION POLICY: ACT FIRST, THINK LATER

27 September 2015

The zeal with which the policy was announced was matched only by the speed with which it was withdrawn. It lasted all of Monday morning to Tuesday evening. Meanwhile, a scapegoat was found—a poor low-level scientist—and everyone else washed his or her hands of the draft National Encryption Policy.

It was indeed a draft, but it was a draft of a national policy that was placed in the public domain to enable stakeholders and the public to offer their comments. Surely, it was approved at a level much above the low-level scientist. Besides, there is the principle of constructive responsibility. Elementary, but it seems to have escaped the minister and the secretary concerned.

This is not the first time that the NDA government has acted first and donned its thinking cap later. Other governments may have also been guilty, but we are concerned with the present, and the tendency to act first and think later raises grave concerns.

BEATING THE RETREAT

The government had been warned on the Land Acquisition Ordinance, but the government went ahead and promulgated the ordinance thrice.

After nine months, it abandoned its misconceived exercise.

The government was warned on 'Net neutrality', but it ignored the warning and ultimately it had to change its position.

At other levels, Maggi noodles was banned, selling and eating beef was banned, meat was banned for several days, and an NGO activist was barred from traveling abroad. In each of those cases, the government concerned was forced to eat humble pie.

The Government of Rajasthan prescribed minimum educational qualifications for candidates in elections to panchayats and municipalities, something that does not apply to candidates in elections to Parliament or the state legislature. One half or more of the electorate was disqualified. Rajasthan got away with holding elections subject to the outcome of the challenge to the new law. But when Haryana tried the same trick, elections have been stopped and the case will be heard soon. The Government of Haryana and the BJP have been warned that the validity of the law is doubtful, but they do not seem to take the warning seriously.

The latest case is the debate on reservation triggered by a conscious statement made by Mr Mohan Bhagwat. The statement was made soon after the three-day 'exchange of views' between the RSS and the government attended by the Prime Minister and senior ministers. It is difficult to believe that reservation was not discussed during the 'exchange of views'. The government hastened to distance itself from Mr Bhagwat's statement, but that was not the end of the story. On the next day, the RSS' view on reservation was faithfully reflected in two Bills passed by the legislature of Rajasthan. The Government of Rajasthan and the BJP have been duly warned that the Bills are vulnerable, but there is no sign that they will heed the warning.

'Act first, think later' has become the leitmotif of the BJP/NDA government. The draft National Encryption Policy is a prime example.

ENCRYPTION: WHOSE RIGHT AND RESPONSIBILITY?

The legal basis claimed is Sections 69 and 84A of the Information Technology Act. They confer power on the government to intercept, monitor or decrypt digital information under certain conditions and to prescribe modes and methods of encryption.

Information—private or public, harmless chatter or highly sensitive—when generated, transmitted, received or stored is encrypted. The key is the encryption codes. Just as a government's encryption codes are the property of the government, encryption codes of service providers like Google, Apple and Facebook are the property of the service providers. Their business depends upon the security of their codes, therefore they constantly innovate, and fight hard to win the perpetual battle between code-makers and code-breakers.

The draft Encryption Policy blithely ignored the realities and challenges of the digital age. It asserted the right of the government to prescribe encryption standards for the three groups of users: government, business and citizens. Vendors of encryption products were obliged to register their products with a government agency and submit working copies of the encryption hardware/software to that agency. Users were mandated to keep information in plain text format for 90 days and make it available, on demand, to law enforcement agencies.

HORRENDOUS CONSEQUENCES

Imagine a government prescribing encryption algorithms for all business and citizen groups! Or imagine the consequences of working copies of all encryption hardware/software available at one place (the designated agency)! Or imagine the risks of keeping plain texts for 90 days! The tribe of hackers, Chinese and others, will be happy men and women.

The authors of the draft policy seem to have no understanding of either security or privacy. Securing information in the digital world is dependent on constant research, innovation, design and application—matters that are best left to vendors, service providers, businesses and citizens. The need for privacy, and the degree of privacy that each citizen desires, are best left to the citizens.

The government's sole concern should be the breach of security of sensitive or classified information. Hence, the government's only right is to prescribe minimum standards of security for different kinds of information and different classes of vendors, service providers and users, and demand that the information be made available if it is connected to a breach of security. I hope the next 'scientist' who will draft the policy will bear these in mind.

POLITICS

LESSONS FOR ALL IN THE DELHI ELECTION

15 February 2015

There is a lesson for everyone in the Delhi election.

THE WINNER

In the campaign, the Aam Aadmi Party (AAP) avoided theatrics and played with a politically straight bat, remained focused on 'bijli, paani and sadak' (electricity, water and roads), and connected with voters belonging to all classes. In government, the people of Delhi will expect the AAP to avoid theatrics and play with a straight bat. Good and bad ideas will come AAP's way, and there are many of both kinds in their manifesto.

The Jan Lokpal, unified transport authority, free Wi-Fi, more schools and colleges, guaranteed education loans, e-rickshaws and some others are good ideas. Halving electricity bills and making Delhi a manufacturing hub are examples of ideas that are half-baked or plain bad.

Mr Kejriwal's biggest problem is the problem of plenty. Seven of the 67 MLAs will become ministers and one the Speaker. How will he keep the remaining members empowered, engaged and on the straight and narrow path?

I sincerely hope that Mr Kejriwal will realise the limitations of the Delhi government and its budget and deliver on his promises one by one. He will make a great beginning if he announces at his swearing-in that, for five years, he will not step out of the boundaries of Delhi—for pleasure or for politics!

THE RUNNER-UP

Strictly speaking, there was no runner-up. We could have called the BJP the Best Loser but for the fact that it made a hash of losing the election. The problem started with the slogan 'Chalo chalein Modi ke saath'. People asked, 'Go where?'. If the BJP worker is honest, she will admit that Mr Modi had made—and continues to make—a number of attractive promises but has not taken the country anywhere near the promised land. Not one Bill of consequence has been passed, not one major scheme has been rolled out, and not one policy initiative has impacted the lives of the people. The kindest comment that one could make is that the BJP government is still in the first year of its term.

There were many people who had queered the pitch for the BJP. Among them were Mr Mohan Bhagwat ('one language, one god, one religion'), Mr Sakshi Maharaj ('four children') and Sadhvi Niranjan Jyoti ('haramzaadon'). During the campaign, more joined the diatribe tribe calling Mr Kejriwal 'anarchist', 'thief', 'monkey' and 'liar'.

What people noticed and resented was not so much the name-calling but the silence of the Prime Minister in the wake of the outbursts, campaigns and attacks that not only targeted the minorities but also insulted the tolerant and liberal average Hindu voter.

The lesson for the Prime Minister is that he cannot look in the other direction or remain silent. The lesson for the BJP is that there is no permanent winner.

THE CONGRESS

I did not say this, Mr P.C. Chacko said this: 'There were no committees at the district, block and ward levels in Delhi.' That is the perfect script to lose an election. The Congress has been mulling over a new script since it lost the Lok Sabha election in May 2014. There is no more time to be lost.

I believe several ideas are on the table. There will always be a numero uno, but it is good to present a picture of a collective leadership. King Arthur had his round table. Secondly, the Congress must constitute or reconstitute the committees at the block level. It is a task that can, starting from scratch, be accomplished in 12 months or less. Thirdly, the Congress must communicate its views to its cadres and to the people every day in Hindi, English and other Indian languages.

The most important lesson for the Congress is that there is no permanent loser.

THE OTHERS WHO DID NOT RUN

These parties learnt their lessons even before the first vote was cast in Delhi. A tiger must guard its own turf and not venture into unknown territory. So, in the foreseeable future, Mr Mulayam Singh and Ms Mayawati must confine themselves to Uttar Pradesh, Mr Nitish Kumar and Mr Lalu Prasad to Bihar and Ms Mamata Banerjee to West Bengal. There is space for each of them in their respective state.

THE COMMUNISTS

Their pride will not allow them to admit it was a huge blunder to withdraw support to the UPA, vote against the UPA government and expel Mr Somnath Chatterjee from the party. Notwithstanding their archaic economic views, the Communists have an important role to play to ensure that the polity of the country leans in favour of the poor. In developed countries the 'poor' will be the 'middle class', and as India develops, the polity must lean in favour of the middle class. It is a mystery to me why the Communists abdicated this duty.

THE VOTER

She teaches lessons. She also learns lessons. She must always remember that she is the class monitor. If the political leader or the government becomes uncaring or self-seeking or arrogant or vain or corrupt, it is because she failed to monitor the class.

ETERNAL VIGILANCE IS THE PRICE OF LIBERTY

15 March 2015

To most Indians, the story of the struggle for Independence ended on 15 August 1947. In fact, the struggle began on that day.

The idea of an open and free society was unknown in most parts of India and to several generations of Indians. Many of them lived their whole lives under a king or a satrap. Many lived their whole lives in fear of God and godmen. Many accepted the societal rules and restrictions as if they were scripture. As a result, we have inherited layer upon layer of dogma, myth, superstition, prejudice and discrimination. Many of us believe, wrongly, that this is our 'culture', and believe, wrongly, that we should be proud of our 'culture'. Dissent has to struggle to find a place in this culture. It is not a culture of tolerance, as we sometimes rationalise, but a culture of intolerance.

In such infertile soil, it is hardly to be expected that liberalism will take roots.

John Stuart Mill, in his book *On Liberty*, proposed a simple principle of liberalism. He wrote, 'the sole end for which mankind are warranted, individually or collectively, in interfering with the liberty of action of any of their number is self-protection. That the only purpose for which power can be rightfully exercised over any member of a civilised community, against his will, is to prevent harm to others.'

Our sense of liberty is the exact opposite. We exercise power over another member of society, against his will, because, as Mill cautioned, we think that it is for 'his own good, …because it will be better for him to do so, because it will make him happier, because, in the opinion of others, to do so would be wise or even right'.

INTOLERANCE ON THE RISE

The rising tide of illiberalism and intolerance is frightening. Look at what is happening around us: ban the book (Wendy Doniger), ban the documentary (*India's Daughter*), ban beef (in Maharashtra). Attack the writer (Puliyur Murugesan), lynch the rape accused (in Nagaland), kill the rationalist (Govind Pansare). Return to your forefather's religion (ghar wapsi), vandalise the church (in Delhi), add the Gita to the syllabus (in Haryana).

The common thread that runs through most of these eruptions is a reactionary ideology, Hindutva. I fear that illiberalism and intolerance are on the rise because the zealots believe that the State is on their side and they can silence the voice of the liberal or the dissenter. They also believe that if they gather sufficient numbers, they will be the 'State' and their word will be the 'law'.

There is another kind of intolerance. The new chairman of the Censor Board believes that it is his duty to ban cuss words in films. The Chief Passport Officer believes that it is his duty to direct that Ms Priya Pillai should be off-loaded if she boarded an aircraft to deliver a talk on human rights violations to a group of British MPs. A duty magistrate believes that he is obliged to pass an ex parte order banning the telecast of an interview with a convict that was recorded with the express permission of the jail authorities. These worthies believe that by doing what they did they will be on the 'right' side of the State.

Let us examine the ban on beef. Let us assume that most Hindus do not eat beef, believe that cow slaughter is heresy, and believe that the cow must be protected even after it has stopped yielding milk. Thus far, there is no issue.

Nearly all Muslims do not eat pork, believe that the pig is an unclean animal, and believe that eating pork is heresy. Here too, there is no issue.

Illiberalism raises its head when we allow people to rule that beef (or pork) shall not be served or sold or eaten. Beef is the poor man's meat. It is a rich source of protein. People belonging to faiths other than Hinduism eat beef. Young Indians, especially in foreign countries, enjoy their hamburger. Pork is the meat of choice in many countries of Europe and East Asia. When a small number of the majority, because it is in government or because it is the Taliban, decides to ban beef or pork, it violates the principle of liberalism.

MAJORITARIANISM WILL FAIL

In most cases, the intolerance is foolish and will be swept away by the force of technology. Thanks to Skype, Ms Priya Pillai did address her audience and, what would have been a little-noticed lecture, became a cause célèbre. Thanks to YouTube, *India's Daughter*, was viewed in millions of homes.

I think we should pause and ask ourselves, 'Can the State really succeed in banning beef without throwing thousands of people out of employment and perhaps hundreds of people in jail?' In the same vein, the Supreme Court should ask itself, 'Can you really prosecute and punish consenting adults for violating Section 377 of the Indian Penal Code?'

Moral majoritarians do not realise the futility or the foolishness of their words and deeds. They also undermine the fundamental principles of an open and free society: diversity, pluralism and choice. They will fail, but the true democrat and liberal must speak up and ensure that the moral majoritarians fail comprehensively.

IT IS THE 'MIDDLE' THAT MAKES OR BREAKS

17 May 2015

I believe that the people of every country have concerns that are broadly similar. And when they vote in an election they vote in a way that is, by and large, similar, at least in democracies.

One set of concerns can be called material concerns. Will there be enough jobs? Will there be a rise in the income and the living standards of average persons? Will there be better law and order and security? Will there be better schools, better hospitals and better roads? These concerns are simple, understandable, uncomplicated and seemingly measurable. Since all political parties promise that everything will be 'better', there is no basis to prefer one party over the other on the strength of their promises alone. It is performance that will count.

On performance, Mr David Cameron's Conservative party government in Britain was rated average. At the same time, few believed that Mr Ed Miliband's Labour party will do better. They were at par. And all pre-election polls showed that the two parties were in a neck and neck race, neither would get an absolute majority, and perhaps the Tories would emerge as the single largest party by a short head.

UNARTICULATED CONCERNS

There is another set of concerns that cannot be easily articulated, and few would even attempt to give expression to those concerns. They are supposedly the domain of the pundits and experts—usually the economists and sociologists. But you will be making a big mistake if you think that these unarticulated concerns are imaginary or that they do not play on the minds of the people. They do. If a party leaned too far to the left ('borrow more, spend more') or too far to the right ('quit the European Union'), it will offend the common sense of the average person. If a party was too dependent on a regional party ('Scottish National Party will not give a free pass to Labour'), it will offend the pride of the average English, Irish and Welsh voter. If a party stoked prejudice or fear ('stop immigration'), it will offend the self-esteem of the average person who regards herself as a broad-minded, tolerant and decent person. She knows such policies will make a difference to the lives of citizens, although she may not be able to articulate how or why.

It is these alternate concerns that propelled the Tories ahead of the other parties and gave them a slender majority of 12 in the House of Commons.

The consensus in Britain was that few really liked the Tories (Mr Cameron was too posh), but the voters liked the other parties and their top leaders even less. At least, Mr Cameron advocated spending within means, a referendum on Britain remaining in the European Union, the merit of a single-party government, and a reasonable limit on the number of immigrants. The Tories may have lost the parochial, the ideological and the xenophobic votes, but they got huge support from the 'middle'. The 'middle' consists of the middle class, the non-ideological voters and those who are proud to describe themselves as average and decent.

THE 'MIDDLE' THAT DECIDES

In developed and fast-developing countries, the only group that is growing is the 'middle'. More people in such countries like to identify themselves with the middle class; even the rich call themselves 'upper middle class'. And among the genuinely poor, many aspire to join the ranks of the middle class. Look back 20 years and look at today: fewer people walk barefoot; a vegetable vendor proudly speaks on her mobile phone; at the first opportunity, a bicycle is replaced by a two-wheeler. The footwear, the mobile phone and the two-wheeler are not signs of wealth, but symbols of an aspiring class. Middle class values, not quite defined, are considered good values. Belonging to the growing and anonymous middle class encourages one to join street protests, engage through the social media, and be critical without being offensive. Throughout the world, it is the middle class that has readily supported green causes, LGBT rights, free speech, and whistleblowers.

The lesson from Britain's election is that a wise political party will embrace the 'middle' or the centre of the political and social spectrum. Even when sections of a party attempt to pull towards the extreme left or extreme right, the leader must resolutely hug the middle.

Mr George Osborne, Chancellor of the Exchequer, once said, 'When in Opposition move to the centre, when in government move the centre.'

A true test of popularity is whether anyone who voted in the election against the party that formed the government after the election has turned into a supporter of that party and the government. Conversely, has anyone who voted for the party turned into an opponent of the government? By this test, more leaders have failed than succeeded. Mr Hollande of France and Ms Rousseff of Brazil are among those who failed. Ms Merkel of Germany passed with high marks. Mr Cameron seems to have made the grade for the present. A more accurate judgment can be made after his government has completed one year in office.

The 'middle' can be very supportive, it can also be unforgiving. It is the 'middle' which makes or breaks governments.

MAGNA CARTA DOES NOT ASSURE LIBERTY

28 June 2015

King John ruled England from 1199 to 1216. He was, by most accounts, an incompetent king. He betrayed almost everyone he could profitably betray, but he overdid his Machiavellian stratagems, losing key allies as a consequence. He was a forgettable king.

Why do we remember him today? Because 800 years ago this month he signed a document called the Magna Carta (the 'Big Charter').

He did not sign the document out of love for liberty or equality. He signed it under duress in order to buy peace with the barons and the bishops. The barons were tyrants who treated their subjects much worse than how the king treated them. The bishops wanted power to dominate all aspects of medieval life. The Magna Carta was a religio-political project of the vested interests to grab power that led to many problems in medieval Europe but, ironically, it is remembered today as the harbinger of modern liberal democracies!

MYTH AND INFLUENCE

Sprinkled across the 63 clauses of the charter are promises that have enduring value. Freedom was promised to religious institutions, but the only religious institution was the Church. Protection of property rights was promised, but only a small number of barons owned land. The charter promised that 'no man shall be seized or imprisoned....except by the lawful judgment of his peers', but only knights and landowners participated in an inquest. The Magna Carta meant little for the vast majority of the people.

However, the myth and influence of the original charter persisted and it was reissued many times over the next few centuries. It is believed to have ushered in the rights-based approach to Constitutional theory. It is acknowledged as the source of the Bill of Rights (1689) that was adopted in England. Lord Denning called the Magna Carta 'the greatest constitutional document of all times—the foundation of the freedom of the individual against the arbitrary authority of the despot'.

There is no date in history on which freedom came in a flood to all the people. It was through relentless struggle that freedom was won by many sections of the people and liberties were extended to more and more persons—sharecroppers, traders, illiterates, women, blacks, indigenous persons, soldiers on duty, prisoners, and overseas citizens.

THREAT OF MAJORITARIANISM

As the arc of freedom has embraced more parts of the world, regrettably, some other parts of the world have regressed into tyranny and loss of liberties. Even liberal democracies have been found to be too willing to impose 'reasonable restrictions' and bend the meaning of what is 'reasonable'. Liberty is a good in itself. You have the liberty to speak, to write, to eat the food you want, to wear the clothes you like, to marry the person you love, and to worship the god you believe in. How can any restriction on that liberty be 'reasonable'? And who will decide what is reasonable and what is not?

If you examine the matter closely, you will find that the so-called 'reasonable restrictions' reflect the will of the so-called 'majority'. But who is the majority? Is it the majority of persons belonging to a caste or a religion? Is it the majority of a neighbourhood or a state or the whole country? The greatest threat to liberty is majoritarianism.

No one can be allowed to take away our liberties by a stroke of the pen. The story of the Emergency is a powerful reminder that such an attempt will fail sooner than later. Thanks to the Magna Carta, the idea of rule of law was born. The rule of law strikes at arbitrariness and enjoins those entrusted with power to use it without fear or favour, ill will or affection.

LIBERTY ERODED BY STEALTH

Liberties are eroded by stealth, by spreading myths, by propaganda and lies, by money power, and by muscle power. Liberties are also eroded by mischievous laws, the mischief often hidden in lofty objectives and legal jargon. Why are the property rights of small farmers (land) less important than the property rights of large corporates (intellectual property)? Why are the environmental and livelihood concerns of forest dwellers less important than the environmental and health concerns of city dwellers? Intimidation of vulnerable voters is an erosion of the hard-won right to vote. Hitler's Germany suppressed liberties by perfecting the art of propaganda and of spreading lies. Watch the movie *Selma*, and you will be horrified to learn that the right to vote was denied to blacks for a hundred years after the American Civil War.

The concept of liberty is expanding. Not all ideas will be universally accepted, yet each one deserves its space and needs to be expressed. Periyar E.V. Ramasamy broke idols and called believers fools, he acquired a large following of atheists, yet theism flourished in Tamil Nadu. Both theism and atheism found their space. Homosexuality was illegal in Ireland (largely Catholic) until 1993, yet the Irish voted this month 62 per cent to 38 per cent to legalize same sex marriage. People's notions of liberty are usually very different from the official view. The answer to bad ideas is good ideas, not a ban on ideas (or beef or books or travel or cuss words in movies) that somebody considers bad.

Liberty is a good in itself and, let me recall the words of wisdom, 'eternal vigilance is the price of liberty'.

THE RISE AND RISE OF INTOLERANCE

6 September 2015

Among the many myths about Indian society is an ancient one—that we are, and have always been, a tolerant society. It is an old yarn to cover the prejudices, discrimination, oppression and violence that have, unfortunately, marked our history.

The intolerance is most pronounced when it comes to matters concerning identity—not religious identity alone, but every kind of strongly-believed identity such as caste, gotra, language and region.

CELEBRATE REFORMERS, JUNK REFORMS

We celebrate the life of a Saint Ramanuja or an E.V. Ramasamy ('Periyar') or a Mahatma Phule or a Raja Ram Mohan Roy. We hold out their lives as examples of how a tolerant Indian society allowed them large space to propagate their views while we conveniently forget the fact that few were actually converted by them to support the causes they espoused. I suspect that celebrating the reformers—while junking the reforms—is a way of atoning for our guilt and shame.

There are temples that still bar the entry of dalits. Every superstition and custom that Periyar campaigned against remains deeply entrenched and practised. In fact, some have acquired pernicious proportions. Time was when a Sikh and a Hindu could love, marry and live happily ever after in Punjab and elsewhere. Marriage between a Christian Nadar and a Hindu Nadar was common in Tamil Nadu. Today, in some parts of India, if a Hindu (boy or girl) is friendly with a Muslim (girl or boy), they are visited with grave consequences. The fact that there are more examples of inter-religious consortium cannot hide the other grim truth that there are many more examples of religious intolerance and persecution.

There is reason to believe that intolerance is on the rise. Look at the number of things that we ban—beef, jeans, books, cuss words, NGOs, websites, Internet services...

Look at the growing exclusiveness—Muslim candidates may not apply for jobs, single women are not welcome as tenants, this apartment building is only for vegetarians...

The intolerance brigades are now organising themselves and mutating into 'movements': ghar wapsi, love jihad...

It is intolerance that brought down the Babri masjid. It is intolerance that proclaims that all history written so far is a left-wing distortion. It is intolerance that finds fault with a thoughtful and insightful speech of Vice President Hamid Ansari that explored the many challenges faced by the Islamic community in India.

INTOLERANCE AND VIOLENCE

Rising intolerance, inevitably, reveals its violent nature. We readily agree that the Taliban and the Islamic State (IS) are intolerant and violent movements that have destroyed priceless monuments (the Bamiyan statues) and heritage sites (Palmyra). But we scarcely notice the violence involved in the attack on churches and pubs, in the excommunication of a young couple or in the expulsion of two students who shared affection.

The growing intolerance is extending to the realm of ideas. Atheism is taboo. Superstitions cannot be questioned. The warrior-king, Shivaji, cannot be portrayed as a secular ruler. Miracles cannot be exposed as fake. Charlie Hebdo cartoons cannot be reprinted in a newspaper. Result: Shireen Dalvi who reprinted the cartoons is bullied, Sanal Edamuruku who exposed a so-called miracle is threatened, and Govind Pansare (who portrayed Shivaji as a secular king), Narendra Dabholkar (who campaigned against superstition) and M.M. Kalburgi (who opposed idolatry) are murdered.

Such acts are in breach of the law, but when such acts are committed with impunity, the issue goes beyond the realm of law and order. It is no longer a question of simply finding the perpetrators, prosecuting them and punishing them according to law. The more important question is, how did these fanatics acquire a sense of being above the law and the Constitution? What gives them the confidence that they can get away with their crimes, they may not be prosecuted at all and, even if they are brought before the law, they can escape deterrent punishment?

UNDERLYING FACTORS

The answer is several-fold: firstly, the State, especially the Executive, has many sympathisers with their cause and is often soft or inept in setting the law in motion.

Secondly, the fanatics believe the law can be bent. Bungling instead of investigation, delayed trial instead of swift justice, fines instead of imprisonment, parole instead of judicial custody, remission instead of serving a sentence, and mercy instead of justice have blotted the administration of law.

Thirdly, they are able to win social support that sometimes turns into support of the whole community or caste. The perpetrators remain anonymous and no one will come forward to expose them.

Fourthly, the punishment of death may bring the halo of martyrdom. There are some people who venerate Indira Gandhi's killers almost at par with Shaheed Bhagat Singh. The destroyers of the Babri masjid are Hindutva heroes. Islamist terrorists are jihadis for whom the gates of heaven are open.

As intolerance rises, liberal thought, pluralism and scientific temper will suffer. The gainer will be polarization. Communities will become more inward-looking, selfish, protective and violent.

The Pansares, the Dabholkars and the Kalburgis can only do so much to bring about change—and sometimes may have to pay the supreme price. Only the State—fearless, strong, secular and fiercely loyal to the Constitution—can stand up to, and roll back, the growing threat of intolerance and violence.

Do you believe that we have, or are building, such a State?

REFUGEES, IMMIGRANTS AND HUMANITY

20 September 2015

As long as humankind has existed, misery has been its companion. Poverty, disease, civilian strife, persecution and wars have brought untold misery to humankind. There is no greater misery than having to flee one's home and hearth and seek refuge in another country whose people may speak a different language or practise a different religion or follow a different culture. According to the United Nations High Commissioner for Refugees, at the end of 2014, there were about 59.5 million persons who had been displaced because of conflict, war or persecution.

Following Partition, India and Pakistan endured the terrible tragedy of mass displacement. Millions of Hindus and Sikhs left Pakistan for India and millions of Muslims left India for Pakistan. It was the last— and the darkest—chapter of our inspiring freedom struggle. Thanks to the statesmanship of Jawaharlal Nehru and Vallabhbhai Patel, India demonstrated its humanity and emerged as a shining example of tolerance, accommodation and generosity. Yet, there were shameful aspects to that story. Neither theocratic Pakistan nor secular India could prevent the killing of thousands of people who were moving from one country to the other.

Many of us have heard first-hand accounts of refugees and how they seized the opportunity and re-built their lives virtually brick by brick. Punjab, Haryana and Delhi abound with examples of refugees who became successful in different walks of life. Two refugees rose to become prime minister of India.

EUROPE'S HUMANITY ON TEST

Europe is no stranger to the phenomenon of refugees. Post World War II, European countries accepted refugees. Europe prospered, and not the least among the reasons for Europe's prosperity was the energy brought by the refugees. They were hardworking, disciplined and ambitious and integrated with the communities in which they had made their new homes.

Despite that history, for some days in the last few weeks, there was despair that Europe had abandoned its humanity, until a wise leader, Ms Angela Merkel, brought sobriety and statesmanship to urge her fellow leaders to find a solution to the problem. The picture of hundreds of Germans holding placards with the word 'Willkommen' and embracing refugees came as a salve to hearts that were devastated by the photograph of three-year old Aylan Kurdi's lifeless body lying face down in the water on the coast of Turkey. Europe, after some anxious weeks, rediscovered its humanity, although there are still some holdouts like Hungary.

MIGRATION IS ANOTHER ISSUE

Quite often, people confuse refugees for immigrants. Refugees are victims who face persecution or death or both in their own countries. They have no choice but to flee their home countries.

Migrants are a different category. They have a choice, and they exercise the choice of leaving their own countries usually in search of better economic opportunities. Many people migrate because of abject poverty or lack of jobs. However, many educated or well-to-do people also migrate. Witness the number of people who emigrate every year from India to the United States, Canada, Australia or New Zealand seeking better education or a better job or a better environment or a better political system in which to live and raise families.

The United States is a nation of immigrants, but there is fierce opposition to immigrants (allegedly illegal) from Mexico and other South American countries. Europe needs immigrants to sustain its economy and support its ageing population. The number required has been estimated at 40 million people over the next five years, but there are governments and right-wing political parties who are spearheading the opposition to immigrants.

The lesson of history is that migration cannot be stopped, it can only be managed. Countries are struggling to find a model for managing migration that would be appropriate to their situation.

NO PLACE FOR PREJUDICE

India has, from time to time, faced the problem of refugees, the most recent being a few thousand from Sri Lanka. Refugees who flee persecution or death must be welcomed regardless of their race or religion. Recently, there was outrage when some countries (Hungary, Australia) sought to give preference to Christian refugees, thus betraying their religious and cultural prejudice. But why was there no outrage when the Government of India formulated a policy to 'exempt Bangladeshi and Pakistani nationals belonging to minority communities from the relevant provisions of the Passport Act and the Foreigners Act'? The press release stated that the policy will apply only to Hindus, Sikhs, Christians, Jains, Parsis and Buddhists. What about Shias, Ahmadis, atheists and rationalists?

When I first visited the India–Bangladesh border, the thought that occurred to me was 'this land was one country, Partition made it two, and liberation made it three'. India's borders are quite porous. India cannot allow itself to be overwhelmed by poor immigrants in search of economic opportunities when a large number of Indians are themselves very poor. In order to manage migration, border fencing is necessary and reasonable border controls must be in place. Time-bound work permits, instead of permanent residency or long-term visas, can be issued liberally but time limits must be enforced strictly. Above all, we can help our neighbours prosper: a prosperous region is the best antidote to mass migration.

Every nation must remain mindful of the distinction between refugees and immigrants. If they do, reasonable solutions can be found to both problems.

WHAT'S AT STAKE IN BIHAR POLLS

11 October 2015

Novelty of elections is passé. Elections will take place, the results will be announced, a party or an alliance will win, a government will be formed, and in a few days life will be back to the usual routine.

However, I have the feeling that after the Bihar election, life in Bihar—and India—will not be back to the usual routine.

I have the feeling that the battle for Bihar is not a battle for capturing power in Bihar but for capturing power to rewrite the narrative of India. The battle for Bihar is not being fought only within Bihar, it is being fought in places such as Muzaffarnagar and Dadri, in states such as Maharashtra and Karnataka, and in the social and traditional media.

THE FOUR-TIER ARRANGEMENT

The central issue in the Bihar elections is no longer the development of Bihar, it is the cow. The cow has become the symbol of the revisionist 'idea of India'. That idea is based on an old history of hierarchy, patriarchy, exclusion, discrimination, violence and majoritarianism.

The historical facts are bitter and brutal. For centuries, Indian society has been structured around varna, a four-tier arrangement that encompassed the majority, but also excluded a large number from

149

the arrangement. The excluded were the outcasts or the untouchables. Inequality by birth was the basis of the arrangement. That inequality could not be changed, it stayed with you throughout your life, and it decided what you will do, what you will have and what you will be. It was the antithesis of 'all men and women are born equal and shall have equality of opportunity'.

Besides, within the arrangement, there were rules in respect of women, marriage, food, clothing, worship, observance of rituals, etc. Violation of the rules was visited with swift punishment—usually exclusion.

The arrangement was challenged from time to time by native-born 'reformers' and by so-called 'invaders'. The reformers were quickly absorbed into the arrangement and many of them were turned into icons. The invaders (who undoubtedly brought different sets of problems) were turned into objects of hate, especially if they practised another faith like Islam or Christianity.

The most powerful challenge to the arrangement was the making of the Constitution of India and the birth of a secular, democratic and liberal republic. It was an excruciatingly slow process, but thanks to the advance of adult suffrage, education, industrialization, urbanization and communication, the arrangement began to crumble. There was hope that India would, after all, become a more equal, just and humane society. We seemed to be learning the enduring lesson of history that only a country organized on the basis of liberty, equality and fraternity could become rich and prosperous.

THE FORCES OF DARKNESS

The ascent to power of the BJP—with an absolute majority in the Lok Sabha—brought with it a sense of foreboding. However, we were assured that, at the helm, was not the RSS but Mr Narendra Modi. We were told to look at Modi 2.0, the Gujarat model, his spoken words, his energy, his enthusiastic embrace of technology, etc. For a while, the nation was impressed by Mr Modi, but questions have begun to be raised.

Why have khap panchayats become more visible and active and

who has allowed them to dispense kangaroo justice? Why is there a mushrooming of vigilante groups and moral police brigades? Why is there a rash of bans—from jeans to books to food to authors to artistes to NGOs? Why is dissent being put down with every instrument of State power? Why have eminent scholars been ousted from academic and cultural institutions? Who killed Dabholkar, Pansare and Kalburgi? Why are communal incidents on the rise (in the first half of 2015 there have been 330 incidents with 51 deaths compared to 252 incidents and 33 deaths in the first half of 2014)? Why do ministers, MPs and MLAs who have sworn to uphold the Constitution speak the language of divisiveness and hate? And, above all, why is the Prime Minister silent?

AN EXISTENTIAL THREAT

Mr Narendra Modi speaks on practically every subject and is usually well briefed, even if he occasionally trips (as he did on India's GDP). He remembers birthdays and he greets sportspersons on winning a tournament. But he is ominously silent on the deliberate attempt to write a counter-narrative to the idea of a modern, secular and liberal India. His silence on the killings of Dabholkar, Pansare and Kalburgi and on the lynching of Akhlaq is unforgivable.

Indian society is more polarized today than at any time since the Partition (1947) and the demolition of the Babri masjid (1992). With the RSS and the BJP working overtime to snatch a victory in Bihar, will polarization be complete after the election? I shudder to think what will happen then. Recall the words of Khushwant Singh in *Train to Pakistan*: 'Both sides killed. Both shot and stabbed and speared and clubbed. Both tortured. Both raped.'

As we wondered how long Prime Minister Modi will remain silent, he broke his eight-day silence only to offer a homily on unity and communal harmony. There was no condemnation of the killings or of the hotheads. There was no warning of action or punishment.

The nation faces a grave existential threat—polarization along religious lines—and, regrettably, we have only Modi 1.0.

A CALL TO THE COLLECTIVE CONSCIENCE

18 October 2015

After many years, 'protest' has found its voice and a new legitimacy. In the last two weeks, about 25 writers have returned their Sahitya Akademi awards and some have resigned from the Akademi.

Most of these writers practise their craft in regional languages. They are quiet, private citizens wrestling with the human condition using the written word. Protesting against the State is not their usual business. Their dignified statements showed how deeply disturbed they are by the general rise of intolerance in the country, the murders of scholars and rationalists, the threats to writers and academics, and the lynching of a poor man by a mob that concluded that he had kept beef in his home. They are appalled—as millions are—by the apathy or connivance of those in authority.

Returning an award is a symbolic act. Rabindranath Tagore, Shivaram Karanth and Khushwant Singh had done so. It does not diminish the work of the author for which the award was given. However, these writers are taking a huge personal risk by publicly taking a stand against the forces of intolerance and their mentors. The writers are also allowing their private spaces to be invaded by persons whose only skill is heaping abuse. They have been accused of opportunism and partisanship. They are asked why they did not protest in the past during times of riots or suppression of rights. One does not lose the right to protest just because one did not express equal outrage over each reprehensible incident. Besides, the accusation is simply not true. Ms Nayantara Sahgal, for instance, resigned from her position at the Sahitya Akademi when the Emergency was proclaimed.

THE COLLECTIVE CONSCIENCE

Ordinary citizens are deeply moved by the call of the writers to the conscience of the country. There is a collective conscience, however tattered it might be due to prejudices triggered by religion, caste and language. That conscience can be stirred by an individual's act of defiance or protest.

In 1930, a frail man, wearing no more than a single unstitched piece of cloth around his waist, bent down and scooped a handful of salt from the ocean.

In 1955, a poor black woman defiantly refused to give up a seat reserved for black people in a public bus.

In 1962, a tall, sturdy man walked into prison with a smile on his lips and remained there for 27 years, resolute and undefeated.

Each of these acts of protest signaled the beginning of a revolution that changed history. India threw out the colonial masters who had ruled for over 200 years and became an independent republic. The United States embarked on a long march to end racial discrimination. South Africa put an end to apartheid and regained its soul as well as civil liberties for its people.

PRESSURE TO CONFORM

We continue to witness solitary acts of defiance, but are we inspired by such acts to ring in the changes that are the goal of the protests? Sadly, the answer is no. Ms Irom Sharmila has refused food for 15 years in support of her demand to repeal the Armed Forces (Special Powers) Act, but both she and her struggle have been largely forgotten. We are not sufficiently moved to bring even minimal amendments to an inhumane law that is a blot on democracy.

The duties of a citizen do not begin and end at the polling booth. Our obligation is not only to vote to office a government. We have a daily obligation to ensure that government fulfils, every day, its raj dharma. There is no instrument more powerful than dissent to keep the rulers in check. In fact, a wise ruler will welcome his critics. As the sage, Tiruvalluvar, said, 'A ruler who has no critics will meet his downfall even if he does not have enemies' (*Kural* 448).

Our social organizations will pressure us to conform, to think in a particular way, to abide by the wishes of the majority. Many of us, unthinkingly, succumb to the myth that a 'strong' (read: dominating) leader is better for the country than a 'soft' (read: consensus-building) leader. Another myth is that rapid economic development can be achieved only by accepting a simple set of ideas around which there should be no debate or dissent (the so-called Singapore model). Yet another myth is that the hallmarks of a great nation are large armed forces, nuclear weapons and meek neighbours. The history of the world tells us that none of these myths is true. On the contrary, open, plural and tolerant societies that were governed by modest and self-effacing leaders have achieved unprecedented prosperity and excellence in many fields.

The writers are protesting against events that have not only political overtones but have profound social consequences. Are all Indians obliged to conform to one notion of religion or food or language or dress? And are all those who do not conform to be 'excluded' from public life, public institutions, public discourse and even public spaces?

A different view—dissent—is the essence of a free society. Suppose Voltaire had said 'I disapprove of what you say and I shall put you to death for having said it.' Would the leader feel just 'saddened'? What the writers are saying is the leader should feel outraged and should quell the dark forces of intolerance and violence.

WIN OR LOSE, MR MODI WILL BE ON TEST IN BIHAR POLLS

8 November 2015

When you read this column on the morning of 8 November, the air will be thick with suspense.

Who will win the election in Bihar is the question uppermost on everyone's mind. There are two principal formations: the NDA led by Mr Narendra Modi and the Grand Alliance led by Mr Nitish Kumar. I think one of the formations will get an absolute majority and will be able to form the government. That, in itself, is good. After a bitter, divisive and corrosive campaign, the people of Bihar deserve a stable government.

Which formation wins the Bihar election will matter not only to the people of Bihar but to all the people of India. The announcement of the final result will be a defining moment in the political history of the country.

PRIME MINISTER OR PRACHAR MANTRI?

The result of the Bihar election will matter most to one person—Mr Narendra Modi. No prime minister before him has campaigned so extensively—and aggressively—in a state election. Mr Modi addressed 26 rallies, some even in block headquarters that had never before witnessed a prime minister addressing a gathering. No wonder that, towards the end of the campaign, the people started referring to Mr Modi as Prachar Mantri.

That, Mr Modi is. He is an unequalled pracharak. He loves to campaign. He loves to hold forth to the people from a high and distant stage because that suits his style of communication—one way, no questions, no interruptions and the front rows packed with ardent supporters. Mr Modi also presumably believes that it is his campaign that won the elections for the BJP in 2014 and subsequently in several states.

Mr Modi threw everything in his armoury into the Bihar election. He threw in money, human resources, advertisements, invectives and innuendos on a scale that was unprecedented. Nothing was out of bounds.

The BJP brought in reservation, the cow and finally Pakistan into the debate. The name of the game was polarization. Everyone who protested against the rising intolerance—from writers to scientists to historians to artistes—was mocked and abused. At the end of the campaign, India must have appeared to the world as more divided and chaotic than ever before.

The casualty was development. Mr Modi claims to have a huge stake in the development agenda. That is the plank on which he had won a historic mandate and that is the promise on which he has delivered so little—especially jobs, infrastructure and prices.

Mr Modi also has a huge stake in keeping his flock together—the BJP, the few allies, the RSS and the Sangh Parivar. He has made no secret of his desire to complete his term and win another term in 2019.

Mr Modi has two choices. He can return to being a whole-time Prime Minister and devote the whole of his time and energy to advance the development agenda. Alternatively, he can be the Prachar Mantri and devote practically the whole of his time to winning elections for the BJP as several states, including Uttar Pradesh, will go to elections in the next 18 months.

What will be good for the country? A victory or defeat for the BJP in Bihar?

IF THE BJP WINS

A win in Bihar could propel the party in either direction. Win and continue with the winning formula of polarization is just as likely as win and return to the development agenda. The choice is Mr Modi's. So far Mr Modi has not revealed why he has not reined in the louts and loudmouths. The question is, can't he or won't he? If the truth is he cannot, because of the omnipresence of the RSS, it will be a calamity. If the truth is he will not, because he is a dedicated swayamsevak, it will be a catastrophe. I fear that a win in Bihar will encourage the BJP to embrace more tightly the agenda of polarization.

IF THE BJP LOSES

On the other hand, a loss in Bihar could also push the BJP in either direction. Again, the choice is Mr Modi's. He could pause, take stock, pull back and steer the party on the path of good governance and development. Alternatively, he could come under pressure to throw off all restraints and adopt the core agenda of Hindutva—enforce a uniform civil code, repeal Article 370, build the Ram temple at Ayodhya, ban altogether the slaughter of cows and sale of beef, rewrite history and textbooks and so on. My view—and this is an optimistic view—is that a defeat in Bihar will have a sobering effect on Mr Modi and the BJP.

If that analysis leaves you in uncertainty and despair, I am sorry. My conclusion is that the result of the Bihar election will not matter as much as Mr Narendra Modi's fundamental beliefs. He has, alternately, portrayed himself as Hindu Hriday Samrat and as Vikas Purush. Who is the real Mr Modi will be known when he takes his first decisive political step after the Bihar election—the Cabinet reshuffle.

The Cabinet reshuffle will be a pointer to the direction that Mr Modi intends to take. Win or lose in Bihar, Mr Narendra Modi will be on test.

THE ETHOS OF INDIA WINS THE ELECTION

15 November 2015

Every student of political science will try to make sense of the outcome of the election in Bihar.

It is easy to make nonsense of the result, as the BJP's Parliamentary Board did, blaming it on the 'arithmetic'. What arithmetic? They added the vote shares of the JD(U), the RJD and the Congress in the Parliament election of 2014—when the JD(U) and RJD contested separately—and concluded that the NDA's vote share was smaller and therefore the BJP/NDA was defeated!

Several obvious questions arise:

1. Was the arithmetic not known before the counting day, and yet why did every BJP leader declare that the party would get an absolute (some said two-third) majority?
2. Does a voter vote for the same party in every election?
3. If arithmetic decided elections, how did the BJP win 22 of the 40 seats in Bihar in the Parliament election of 2014? Going by the vote shares in the Assembly election of 2010, the BJP should have won less seats than the JD(U) in 2014.

THE CHANGE SINCE 2014

The answer lies in the change that has taken place in the BJP since 2014, a change that Mr L.K. Advani, Mr M.M. Joshi, Mr Shanta Kumar and Mr Yashwant Sinha described as the 'emasculation' of the party.

In 2014, the BJP presented itself as a democratic party with a collective leadership (although it was subservient to the RSS). Even after he was anointed as the candidate for prime minister, Mr Modi usually deferred to his colleagues. He resolutely and unwaveringly stuck to the theme of development. There was no mention of reservation or the cow or uniform civil code or rewriting history or banning beef, books, jeans or love. In short, the BJP's campaign, spearheaded by Mr Modi, did not challenge or run counter to the ethos of the Indian people. The BJP seemed to respect Indian society's diversity, pluralism and tolerance of differences among the people.

True, there were incidents of intolerance in the run-up to the elections, but few blamed the BJP for those incidents. Even when the extreme right wing of the Sangh Parivar was the provocateur, the BJP's leadership was absolved. In 2014, throughout the period of the election to the Lok Sabha and, subsequently, elections to the legislatures of Maharashtra, Haryana, Jammu & Kashmir and Jharkhand, the BJP seemed to be in sync with the ethos of India. The fear of a fundamentalist right-wing party assuming power receded. The electorate warmed up to Mr Modi and his eloquence and gave him a mandate that no party had got in 30 years.

THE MISTAKES THAT WERE MADE

In the Delhi Assembly election, the BJP made its first mistakes, and paid a price. Those were tactical mistakes like projecting Mr Modi as the face of the next government in Delhi and, later, projecting Ms Kiran Bedi, a new entrant, as the chief minister.

In Bihar, the mistakes were compounded by challenging the very idea of India and allowing the extreme elements to ridicule the idea and its flag bearers ('Abdul Kalam was a nationalist despite being a Muslim',

'Mr Shah Rukh Khan may live in India, but his heart is in Pakistan', 'the return of awards by writers is a manufactured protest').

Take the statement that Mr Modi made after some bombs exploded at Gandhi Maidan, Patna, during a rally in October 2013. Mr Modi asked, with feeling, should Hindus fight Muslims or should they fight poverty; should Muslims fight Hindus or should they fight poverty? It was considered high-minded and placed Mr Modi above the fray. After the murder of Akhlaq, and after many days of silence, Mr Modi made the same statement in October 2015. This time it sounded hollow and left Mr Modi at the centre of a bitter battle.

What was eloquence in 2014 sounded like empty rhetoric in 2015. What were considered credible promises in 2014 appeared to be just chunavi jumla (election theatrics) in 2015.

WHAT A PM CANNOT DO

Who contributed most to the dramatic change of perception?

I am afraid it was Mr Modi himself with liberal help from Mr Amit Shah. As the candidate in 2014, Mr Modi spoke like a prime minister. As the Prime Minister in 2015, he spoke like a candidate. When there was a backlash following Mr Mohan Bhagwat's call to review reservation, Mr Modi repeatedly referred to his caste as ati pichhda (extremely backward). When the slogan of 'Bihari or Baahari' caught on, Mr Modi ridiculed Bihar for its poverty, illiteracy and crime.

A prime minister cannot sound like a stump speaker at a municipal election. A prime minister cannot identify himself with a caste. A prime minister cannot refuse to empathise with a state and its people. A prime minister cannot accuse a chief minister of shielding terrorists.

Mr Modi addressed election rallies in 26 constituencies. The BJP lost in 13. The BJP drew a blank in 13 out of 38 districts of Bihar. It was a crushing defeat. The ethos of India had won.

All is not lost for the central government. As I had said before the election, Mr Modi can 'pause, take stock, pull back and steer the party on the path of good governance and development'. Will he, won't he or can't he? Your guess is as good as mine.

LEGISLATION

STAND UP AND BE COUNTED

18 January 2015

The Right to Fair Compensation and Transparency in Land Acquisition, Rehabilitation and Resettlement Act, 2013 (LARR Act), was not passed in a hurry. It was passed 60 years too late, but nearly unanimously with the support of the BJP.

The main purpose of the LARR Act was to repeal the Land Acquisition Act, 1894 (the old Act). The old Act was an oppressive colonial law that gave unbridled powers to governments to acquire, through legal coercion, any land, from any person, at any time, for any 'public purpose' (so-called). The only obligation under the old Act was to pay one-time compensation to the land owner. The fundamental premise of the old Act was that acquisition for a public purpose was 'good' and opposition to it was 'bad'.

Mercifully, our notions of good and bad are changing.

It is no longer considered good to acquire any land, especially if the land was multi-crop agricultural land, forest land or a tribal habitat; or to ignore the rights of the non-owners who depend on that land for their livelihood; or to acquire land for purely private gain; or to pay only one-time compensation to the land owner.

THE MIDNIGHT ORDINANCE

Shockingly though, our notions of good and bad seem to have changed again within a year of passing the LARR Act. That can be the only explanation for the ordinance that was promulgated on 31 December 2014.

Let me begin by listing the positives in the ordinance. The LARR Act did not apply to acquisition of land under thirteen specified enactments, subject, however, to an ambiguous provision to notify the application of certain provisions (Section 105). The ordinance unambiguously applies the first, second and third Schedules of the LARR Act to such acquisitions too. The ordinance corrects the excessive zeal of Section 87 of the LARR Act that deemed the head of the department to be guilty if an offence under the Act had been 'committed by any department'. The ordinance also corrects two drafting errors.

I have tried but failed to find any more positives in the eleven-clause ordinance. However, there are many negatives.

ASSAULT ON THE SOUL

The soul of the LARR Act is the Social Impact Assessment: does the project for which land will be acquired serve any public purpose and do the social costs and the adverse social impacts of the project outweigh the potential benefits? The LARR Act itself had dispensed with Social Impact Assessment in the case of irrigation projects (proviso to Section 6, sub-section 2) and in cases where the government decided to invoke the 'urgency' provision (Section 40). Moreover, in a case of 'urgency', everything may be dispensed with, including Social Impact Assessment, Rehabilitation and Resettlement, consultation with local bodies, enquiry, and consent of the affected families in cases of acquisition for private companies or public-private partnership projects.

The ordinance goes further and launches an assault on the soul of the LARR Act. A new Section 10A has been added. It lists the projects that will be entitled to special treatment and these are:

- Projects concerning national security, defence and defence production;
- Rural infrastructure including electrification;
- Housing for the poor;
- Industrial corridors; and
- Infrastructure and social infrastructure projects including most public-private partnership projects.

Social Impact Assessment may be excluded in the above cases. The consent of the affected families will not be required. Irrigated multi-crop land may be acquired.

The fundamental premise of a land acquisition law is 'public purpose'. Absent a public purpose, there can be no compulsory acquisition of land. Section 10A has carved out an exception for projects intended to achieve certain public purposes. Can we visualise any project that falls outside the list contained in Section 10A? I dare say that every significant case of land acquisition can be brought within one of the categories in Section 10A and thus spared Social Impact Assessment. That is the terrible mischief wrought by the ordinance.

The ordinance inflicts more wounds. Private hospitals and private educational institutions, even if for-profit, will qualify as infrastructure projects. The LARR Act stipulated that acquisitions under the old Act, delayed by more than five years or where compensation had not been paid, shall lapse (Section 24, sub-section 2). Thanks to the ordinance, few old cases will lapse. Further, the LARR Act required that the acquired land, if it remained unutilised for five years, shall be returned to the land owner (Section 101). The ordinance enlarges the time to the 'period specified for setting up' the project, leaving it vague and open-ended.

STAND UP, BE COUNTED

The ordinance tilts the LARR Act in favour of the promoter of the project and against the land owner, usually a farmer, thus annulling the very purpose of the law.

Every new law must be revisited after a year or two to deal with the practical problems faced during its implementation, and the LARR Act is no exception, but the method adopted (midnight ordinance) and its content (anti-land owner) deserve to be roundly condemned.

Are you for or against the ordinance? It is time to stand up and be counted.

LAND ACQUISITION: NINE STEPS TO NIRVANA

12 April 2015

It is difficult to believe that a government will stake so much—risk of defeat in the Rajya Sabha, political capital, support of allies, the Prime Minister's time—on a mere land acquisition amendment Bill. It is also difficult to believe that the government has decided to brave farmers' anger, street protests and media criticism to get the amendment Bill passed by Parliament. But that is how the story is unfolding.

Prime Minister Modi is leading the government's campaign in support of the Bill to amend the Right to Fair Compensation and Transparency in Land Acquisition, Rehabilitation and Resettlement Act 2013 (LARR Act). Mr Venkaiah Naidu, Minister of Urban Development, gives a byte a day. Mr Arun Jaitley, Minister of Finance, is confrontational one day and conciliatory the next. Mr Birender Singh, Minister of Rural Development (who will pilot the Bill) is, for the most part, silent. Reports indicate that the RSS and its affiliated organizations are divided on the Bill.

The old Land Acquisition Act of 1894 was an oppressive and exploitative colonial legislation. It took free India 66 years to repeal that Act and pass a law that was vastly superior in terms of fairness and justice to the many stakeholders. That the law was passed nearly unanimously, with the support of the principal Opposition party (BJP), was a tribute to the collective wisdom of Parliament.

It, therefore, came as a bolt from the blue that the new government, within six months of coming into office, took up amending the LARR Act as one of its priorities. The government advised the President to promulgate an ordinance on the midnight of 31 December 2014.

I commented on the ordinance in a column that was published in the *Indian Express* on 18 January 2015 (Stand Up and Be Counted). My argument was that dispensing with Social Impact Assessment and the 'consent' clause, in practically every significant case of land acquisition, was an assault on the soul of the LARR Act.

NINE CHANGES IN THE BILL

As opposition to the ordinance mounted, the government brought nine changes in the Bill to replace the ordinance. The government's ministers swore that every concern had been addressed and it was the duty of every patriotic Indian to support the Bill. The Bill was passed by the Lok Sabha but faced fierce opposition in the Rajya Sabha. In the absence of a replacement Bill passed by both Houses of Parliament, the ordinance lapsed on 5 April 2015.

Playing with high stakes, the government has promulgated an ordinance once again. The new ordinance is the old ordinance plus the nine changes. The nine changes have been trumpeted as if they were nine steps to nirvana!

As far as I can recall, no minister of the government has bothered to tell us what these nine changes are. I therefore decided to do a clinical dissection of the nine changes and here is what I found.

COSMETIC AND SUBSTANTIVE

Three changes are cosmetic, nothing has been changed. In the crucial Section 10A, there was an exclusionary clause for 'infrastructure and social infrastructure projects'. Now, the phrase 'social infrastructure' has been dropped. But the word 'infrastructure' remains and the exclusion remains. Secondly, in Section 24, the word 'account' has been replaced by the words 'designated account'. Thirdly, the language of Section 87 has been recast, but the requirement of obtaining sanction before a court may take cognisance of an offence is intact.

Three changes are exhortatory. The government has been told to ensure that only the bare minimum land required for an infrastructure project is acquired. The government has also been directed to prepare and maintain a record of the wasteland it owns. And, finally, the LARR Authority that will hear objections to the land acquisition or to the award of compensation has been required to hold its hearing in the district where the land is located!

Only three changes may be called substantive:

1. The amendment favouring 'private hospitals and private educational institutions' has been dropped.
2. In the case of land acquisition for industrial corridors, Social Impact Assessment and the 'consent' clause will be dispensed with only if land up to one kilometre on either side of the corridor is acquired. Actually, this will complicate matters because two procedures have to be followed in case land up to and beyond one kilometre is acquired.
3. Section 31 sub-section (2) clause (h) has been amended to require that the award shall include particulars of mandatory employment to at least one member of each affected family. This is an improvement upon existing clause (h) and makes explicit what was earlier implicit.

CORE OBJECTION REMAINS

We may welcome the three substantive changes, but what about the core objection to the attempt to re-write a law that came into force only on 26 September 2013? The soul of the LARR Act is Social Impact Assessment. The protection for the landowner (invariably a small landowner) is in obtaining the consent of 70 per cent or 80 per cent of the affected families. The government has made it clear that it cares little for these provisions and is happy to throw them overboard.

Those who stood up to be counted must stand firm. Those who gave the government the benefit of doubt must now stand up and be counted.

EVEN TO THE CAUSING OF DEATH

3 May 2015

Some things do not have a place in a civilised country. One of them is the Armed Forces (Special Powers) Act, 1958 (AFSPA).

AFSPA is unique in many respects. I cannot recall any other law made by Parliament which applies only to the Seven Sisters of the North East—Arunachal Pradesh, Assam, Manipur, Meghalaya, Mizoram, Nagaland and Tripura. In 1990, Parliament passed a similar law that would apply to Jammu & Kashmir.

BLOW TO JURISPRUDENCE

It is a short Act: there is a section containing the definitions and three sections that constitute the essence of AFSPA. The contents of the three sections knock out every cherished principle of criminal jurisprudence.

Section 3 enables the governor of the state (one of the eight) or the central government to declare the whole or part of the state as a 'disturbed area'. Once it is so declared, armed forces can be used in such area 'in aid of the civil power'.

'Armed Forces' means the Army, the Air Force, and the central armed police forces (Central Reserve Police Force [CRPF], Border Security Force [BSF], Indo Tibetan Border Police Force, Central Industrial Security Force).

No time limit has been prescribed for the continuance of the declaration: hence the Supreme Court stepped in and ruled in the case of *People's Movement of Human Rights* that there should be a review of the declaration before the expiry of six months.

Once the armed forces are deployed, they will enjoy special powers conferred under Section 4. Not only superior officers, but any 'non-commissioned officer' (and that includes a jawan) will enjoy such special powers. Here is a summary of the special powers:

1. Suppose an order is promulgated and assembly of five or more persons is prohibited. Anyone on the scene will be 'acting in contravention of any law or order'. Normally, that person can be arrested. But, in a disturbed area, armed with special powers, the officer may, if he thinks it is necessary, fire upon the person even to the causing of death.
2. The officer may destroy any shelter or structure from which armed attacks are likely.
3. The officer may arrest, without warrant, any person against whom the officer has a reasonable suspicion that he has committed or is about to commit a cognizable offence and may use such force as may be necessary to make the arrest.
4. The officer may enter any premises, without warrant, to recover any person, property, arms or ammunition and may use such force as may be necessary.

Section 5 requires that any person arrested shall be brought to the nearest police station with the least possible delay. Note the differences from the normal criminal procedure. Not before a magistrate, but to a police station. Not within 24 hours, but with the least possible delay.

IMMUNITY OR IMPUNITY?

Section 6 gives immunity against prosecution. Such provisions are increasingly questioned because they encourage the armed forces to act with impunity.

There is a widespread belief that even normal police powers are misused. Warrants are not obtained. Reasons are not recorded. Indiscriminate arrests are made. Arrested persons are detained in police stations without any record and are produced before a magistrate long after 24 hours of arrest. Torture is not uncommon. Confessions are extracted.

Imagine the fears of the people in a disturbed area where even a newly-recruited jawan enjoys the 'special powers'. Imagine also a situation where the jawan is working under stress—long hours, little rest, darkness, threat of a terrorist or mob attack, etc. It is a made-to-order situation for an explosion, and that is what is happening—and what happened—where AFSPA is in force.

The demand to repeal AFSPA is not a demand of the separatists in Jammu & Kashmir alone. It has resonance among a cross-section of the people in the eight states as well as across the country. It has the support of academics, lawyers, non-government organizations and human rights groups. The Justice Jeevan Reddy Committee recommended its repeal and the Justice J.S. Verma Committee underlined the 'imminent need to review the continuance of AFSPA'. Ms Irom Sharmila has been on a fast for 14 years demanding its repeal.

TRIED, BUT FAILED

As Home Minister, I was convinced that AFSPA deserved to be repealed. Many senior officers of the CRPF and BSF agreed that they could discharge their responsibilities just as well without AFSPA. I proposed repeal; the Ministry of Defence and the defence forces opposed repeal, and the Defence Minister was unwilling to overrule them. A compromise was struck to amend the law. The National Security Adviser and I drafted the amendments. The most important one was to replace the offending words in Section 4(a) by the words 'use such minimum force as may be necessary'. Other amendments were regarding classifying arrests and searches into cases requiring a warrant and cases not requiring a warrant; and producing a person arrested before a magistrate within 24 hours, excluding the time for travel.

Alas, there was no decision on bringing an amendment Bill. Hence, we continue to live with a draconian law and aid, unwittingly, the campaign of the separatists. We are objects of ridicule among those who value and uphold human rights.

If there is one action that can bring about a dramatic change of outlook from Jammu & Kashmir to Manipur, it is the repeal of AFSPA, and its replacement by a more humane law.

GOVERNMENT PROPOSES, RBI DISPOSES

10 May 2015

An extraordinary thing happened ten days ago, thanks to the Finance Minister, Mr Arun Jaitley. It was even more extraordinary that there was neither praise nor criticism from the Opposition benches. It was as if what had happened was a non-event.

In fact, the two subjects were of great importance as acknowledged by Mr Jaitley himself. The first was taking away the management of the domestic debt of the government from the Reserve Bank of India (RBI) and entrusting it to an independent Public Debt Management Agency (PDMA). The second was moving the regulation of government securities from the RBI to the Securities and Exchange Board of India (SEBI).

Mr Jaitley had endorsed the two ideas. He had included provisions in the Finance Bill to give effect to them. Then, on 23 April, just before the Finance Bill was taken up for consideration and passing, he withdrew those provisions, even while asserting that the two ideas had strong merit!

CONSISTENT SUPPORT FOR PDMA

Let's examine the idea of PDMA. The government borrows to finance its debt. It issues—or authorises the RBI to issue on its behalf—government securities. Who is the largest trader of government securities? RBI. There is an exchange, a depository and a clearing house for government securities. Who is the operator of the securities infrastructure? RBI. There is a vibrant market for government securities. Who is the regulator of the market? RBI. Banks are the largest purchasers of government securities. Who is the regulator of banks? RBI. Government securities are attractive to both sellers and buyers because they carry attractive rates of interest. Who determines the interest rates? RBI, while performing its functions as the monetary policy authority. If there was a case of 'he was judge, jury and prosecutor', this was the best example! The present system is riddled with conflicts of interest that will be obvious to any one who understands markets.

RBI was among the first to recognise the conflicts of interest and, therefore, in its Annual Report 2000–01, proposed the idea of a PDMA. It was supported by the Percy Mistry Committee on Making Mumbai an International Financial Centre (2007), the Raghuram Rajan Committee on Financial Sector Reforms (2008), the Jahangir Aziz Internal Working Group on Debt Management (2008), and the Financial Sector Legislative Reforms Commission (2011). The reports of the two last named bodies also suggested a draft law to create the PDMA.

In the budget for 2007–08, we announced the setting up, in the government, of a Middle Office of PDMA. It was set up and, with the help of RBI's experts, began to acquire skills in public debt management. Mr Jaitley, in his budget for 2015–16, announced the final step of establishing, by law, the PDMA. It was a fine example of continuity in policy.

SEBI AS THE REGULATOR

The other idea of entrusting the regulation of government securities to SEBI also flowed from the conflicts of interest that I have referred to. SEBI is the regulator of the capital market (equity and corporate debt) and will be, shortly, the regulator of the commodities derivatives market as well. It is therefore logical that the government securities market should also be placed under SEBI, which will be the unified regulator of financial trade— an idea supported by the committees mentioned earlier. No one doubts that SEBI has the relevant skills to take on the additional responsibility. Besides, firms and individuals involved in trading will benefit from a single-source and consistent regulation of different kinds of securities.

If the Finance Bill had passed with the original provisions, one body that had authority over the two subject matters would have yielded that authority to other bodies. That body was the RBI. So, Mr Jaitley should tell us if it was indeed the RBI that pressured him to withdraw the provisions.

DUTY TO EXPLAIN

Dr Rajan is the Governor of RBI. He chaired a committee that supported the two reforms. Even a few weeks ago, he publicly backed an independent PDMA. If the RBI that he heads is now opposing the reforms—proposed through statutory changes—he is obliged to disclose the RBI's reasons and also explain why he changed his own views. Equally, Mr Jaitley is obliged to explain why he gave in to RBI's opposition, what is the 'further consultation' with RBI expected to yield, and what is the timeline for the next move on the two proposals.

The two proposed reforms were bold steps that would have brightened a mediocre record of the NDA government as it draws close to the completion of one year in office. The government stood on solid ground. Every committee and commission that had looked into these matters had endorsed the two ideas. The two reforms were consistent with international best practices. The two reforms would not have impacted the average voter and no political capital would have been spent. Yet the government beat a retreat without an explanation.

The Finance Bill would have been passed easily in the Lok Sabha where the government has an absolute majority. There was no fear of the Bill being scuttled in the Rajya Sabha which can only return a Finance Bill. The moral of the story is that numbers alone do not assure economic reforms.

HISTORY IN THE MAKING: THE GST BILL

14 June 2015

We are witnesses to history in the making. The question is: will it be made?

In the budget speech of 2005–06, I had set the goal of a Goods and Services Tax (GST). The GST proposal has had a bumpy ride. The irony is that everyone agrees that a GST is necessary, but cannot agree upon the scope, form and content of the GST.

THE PROMISE OF ARTICLE 301

The fundamental objective of GST is to redeem the promise of Article 301 in Part XIII of the Constitution of India: 'Subject to the other provisions of this Part, trade, commerce and intercourse throughout the territory of India shall be free.'

But the reality is different.

The history of inter-state trade and commerce in India is a sordid story of discriminatory taxes, undue preferences, trade and non-trade barriers, entry tax, octroi, and checkposts. A newcomer would have thought that India was not one republic but a continent that consisted of many independent republics. The central government and the state governments used their powers of taxation to the hilt. They may have had good reasons to do so, but they failed to see that fewer and lower taxes would actually yield more revenue than numerous stiff taxes.

GST is intended to sweep away many taxes. An ideal GST should subsume central excise duty, service tax, additional duties of excise, additional and special additional duties of customs, and central surcharges and cesses. It should also subsume state taxes such as VAT, sales tax, entertainment tax and entry tax not levied by local bodies, luxury tax, taxes on lottery, betting and gambling, tax on advertisements, and state surcharges and cesses. An ideal GST should also apply to all goods and services with nil or very few exemptions.

After a tortuous journey of nearly six years, the UPA government introduced the Constitution (115th Amendment) Bill in March 2011.

Despite a report of the Standing Committee, largely supportive and helpful, the Bill was opposed by some state governments, mainly BJP governments, including Gujarat's. Hence the Bill could not be passed and it lapsed on the dissolution of the 15th Lok Sabha.

THE U-TURN AND THE BILL

Thankfully, the BJP did a U-turn and became an ardent supporter of GST. The BJP government introduced the Constitution (122nd Amendment) Bill in December 2014. It differed from the earlier Bill on many crucial aspects. Nevertheless, there was a Bill, it was a good starting point, it was possible to forge a consensus either in the Standing Committee or on the floor of Parliament, and pass it in both Houses.

Alas, that did not happen. The Standing Committee was by-passed and the Bill was pushed through the Lok Sabha where the BJP has an absolute majority. As expected, it ran into a wall in the Rajya Sabha where the BJP does not have a majority and has landed where it should have landed in the first place—a committee, this time a Select Committee.

Here are some issues for the Select Committee. The path to a good Bill—and passage of the Bill—lies in a satisfactory resolution of these issues:

1. What is the indicative aggregate rate of GST (central GST plus state GST)? It is whispered it will be 26 to 28 per cent, which is exorbitant.

The GST Council will recommend the rates, including floor rates and bands. In my view, it should be not more than 18 per cent.

2. What are the taxes that will be continued alongside GST?
3. What are the excluded goods and services? I can understand alcoholic liquors being kept out, but why exclude petroleum products, tobacco and electricity?
4. Have the states agreed to dismantle all checkposts and entry barriers before a stipulated date?
5. Is the IT backbone to support the administration of GST fully ready and in place?

THREE MORE ISSUES

There are three other issues that merit mention separately. The first is Section 18 of the Bill. This provision imposes an additional tax of not more than 1 per cent on goods in the course of inter-state trade that will be assigned to the states (note the plural). It will be for two years, the provision reads, or for such period as the GST Council may recommend. This is a retrograde provision and negates the very character of GST of a destination-based tax. The Chief Economic Adviser, Dr Arvind Subramanian, has criticised the provision. Section 18 must go.

Secondly, the Bill leaves the dispute resolution mechanism to be decided by the GST Council later. It should be spelt out in the Bill.

The third issue is the date of effect of GST which, under the Bill, is 1 April 2016. The Bill before Parliament is only the amendment to the Constitution. It must be followed by a fleshed-out GST Bill and then by GST rules and regulations. Trade and industry need to invest in IT to comply with the new regime. Stakeholders, down to the common citizen, must be educated on GST. Nothing has happened so far in these areas. Nothing will be lost if a new date is fixed, allowing sufficient time for everyone to get fully ready.

We are on the cusp of the most important structural transformation of the indirect tax system. Let us not flunk the test.

AN OPEN LETTER IN REPLY TO THE FINANCE MINISTER

9 August 2015

Dear Finance Minister,

When the spoken word fails (in Parliament), the written word takes over in a blog! I welcome the opportunity to respond to the letter posted on your Facebook page.

I am glad you have recalled the origin and history of the idea of a Goods and Services Tax (GST). I thank you for this gesture because many BJP leaders and MPs believe that all good things began only on 26 May 2014! However, you have blacked out an important chapter of GST's history. GST was blocked for nearly seven years by an obdurate BJP. The opposition was led by the Finance Ministers of Gujarat (Mr Saurabh Patel) and Madhya Pradesh (Mr Raghavji). Neither the erudite Dr Asim Dasgupta (FM, West Bengal) nor the suave Mr Sushil Modi (FM, Bihar), the first and second chair of the Empowered Committee of Finance Ministers, could persuade the two states to give up their unreasoned opposition to an important reform.

NOT CARVED ON STONE

Nevertheless, we reached a stage where the Empowered Committee submitted its recommendations and Mr Pranab Mukherjee introduced a

Constitution Amendment Bill. It was a sub-optimal Bill. After I took over as Finance Minister in August 2012, I resumed the efforts to improve the Bill, but Gujarat and Madhya Pradesh continued to oppose the reform—and were joined by Tamil Nadu. It is therefore wrong to say that the 'acceptance' of the Empowered Committee's recommendations or the 'Bill' introduced in 2011 was the last word on the subject or that it reflected the final, considered view of the UPA government or of the Congress party.

As you correctly record, your government continued the negotiations and made certain changes to the Bill. It is the contents of the amended Bill—its strengths and weaknesses—that are being debated now and not the contents of an earlier version as if the earlier version had been carved on stone.

MAJORITARIAN APPROACH

Your letter pointedly refers to the dissent note submitted by three members of the Congress, and rebukes them. In fairness, you should have also referred to the dissent notes of Mr A. Navaneethakrishnan (AIADMK) and Mr K.N. Balagopal (CPI[M]). From the tenor of your letter, it appears that you do not intend to engage them in further discussion but will try to ride roughshod over the Opposition and push the Bill through the Rajya Sabha. Nothing can be more fatal to the Bill than the majoritarian approach that you plan to adopt. It is sad that your government has not realised the folly of the majoritarian approach even after the fiasco of the ill-conceived ordinance to amend the Land Acquisition, Rehabilitation and Resettlement Act, 2013.

I hope there still is room for debate and persuasion. It is with that hope that I respond to your criticism of the major points in the dissent note of the Congress.

ENGAGE IN DEBATE

(1) A ceiling may be fixed for the GST rate in the Constitution: You have conceded that 'there may be some rationale in the rate

recommended by the Congress party', but you oppose fixing the rate in the Constitution because it is not 'usually' done. Ironically, you have 'fixed' a rate of 1 per cent for the additional tax in the same Bill! There is also the example of Article 276 (2) that fixes a ceiling of Rs 2,500 per annum on taxes on professions. So, without resorting to specious arguments, let's debate the merits of fixing a ceiling—or a floor and a ceiling—for GST which is an indirect tax and therefore regressive and, hence, warrants placing some restrictions on the rate.

(2) The 1 per cent additional levy is trade-distorting and should be dropped and the word 'supply' occurring in clauses 9 and 18 should be defined: The additional levy is a new provision that was not debated earlier. It has been criticised by the Select Committee as 'likely to lead to cascading of taxes'. The Chief Economic Adviser had called the additional tax retrograde. So, why not drop the additional levy? If you cannot because you may have made promises to some states, what is the difficulty in defining the word 'supply' to keep out intra-firm transfers? You seem to agree on the undesirability of the additional tax, yet you are unwilling to limit the damage that will be caused by it, and I wonder why!

(3) Provide for a Disputes Settlement Authority in the Bill as proposed in 2011: It is baffling that the Bill assigns the function of dispute settlement to the GST Council in which the disputants will be members! Clause 11 of the proposed Article 279A is woefully inadequate. It stipulates that the GST Council 'may decide about the modalities to resolve disputes arising out of its recommendations'. But who will decide the disputes? Who will decide disputes arising not out of the Council's recommendations but otherwise? Dispute resolution is a judicial function and there must be an independent body that will resolve disputes relating to GST.

The other points of disagreement are less important and, if the major disagreements are resolved, they can be resolved too. The starting point must be abandoning the majoritarian approach and willingness to sit across the table with the principal Opposition party that originally proposed the transformational reform.

With regards,
Yours sincerely,
P. Chidambaram

THE NJAC CONUNDRUM

1 November 2015

Imagine that we are citizens of a nation that has just won independence and tasked to write a new Constitution. Imagine we are now drafting the chapter relating to the judiciary.

The main questions that will arise are (1) How will we secure the independence of the judiciary? (2) Who would qualify to be judges? (3) How will the judges be selected and appointed? (4) What will be the powers of the court, especially the superior courts at the national and state levels?

Let us focus on the third question. Should judges be selected by the Executive or a collegium (of judges) or a National Judicial Appointments Commission (NJAC)?

The Constituent Assembly that approved the draft Constitution of India in November 1949 made the following provision:

Article 124: Every judge of the Supreme Court shall be appointed by the President... after consultation with such of the judges of the Supreme Court and of the High Courts in the States as the President may deem necessary for the purpose.

Article 217 is a similar provision for appointments to the High Courts.

JUDGES DON'T APPOINT JUDGES

In the United States, the Executive (the president) has the power to appoint but 'by and with the advice and consent' of the Legislature (the Senate). In both Australia and Canada, it is the Governor General (read: the prime minister) who appoints the judges. Serving judges, including the chief justice, have no say in the appointments.

It is nobody's case that the US, Australia and Canada do not have independent judiciaries. Nor can anyone argue that the judges of the Supreme Court of India appointed before 1993 (when the collegium was invented) were not independent.

No system of appointment is perfect. The collegium, that was vigorously defended by four out of the five judges who declared the NJAC Act illegal, has its faults. So said all the five judges, and they have posted the case for further hearing on 3 November 2015.

In no country of the world do serving judges exclusively select and appoint judges. In the Indian context, it may be conceded that the Executive should not have the exclusive authority to appoint judges. The judiciary too must have a role. Some say the judges must have a predominant role, some contend that Parliament must 'advise and consent', but the judges have argued—and now held—in favour of exclusive authority to themselves.

PREMISES AND COROLLARIES

There are four fundamental premises underlying the judgement in the NJAC case, and each has a corollary. Firstly, exclusive authority of the judges is essential to protect the independence of the judiciary (corollary: participation, even minimal, of the Executive or civil society will compromise judicial independence). Secondly, no one outside the judiciary has the wisdom to assess the ability and suitability of a person to be appointed as a judge (corollary: judges always do an outstanding job of selecting new judges). Thirdly, civil society cannot offer two eminent persons to participate in the selection process (corollary: once appointed, judges are evolved members of the human race that sets them apart from the rest). Fourthly, politicians are corrupt and unworthy (corollary: judges are incorruptible).

There may be a grain of truth in each of these premises; there is absolutely none in the corollaries. The judgement (4:1) in the NJAC case is the latest episode in the long-running drama of institutional mistrust. It is a pity that our institutions are wary of other institutions but generous in self-assessments!

NJAC ACT FLAWED

Sober reflection will lead to the conclusion that the predominant role may belong to the Chief Justice of India (and the collegium), but there must be checks and balances and the Executive also must have a role.

In that view, the 99th Constitution Amendment was indeed a valid law, but the NJAC Act was flawed: non-definition of 'eminent persons', veto for any two members, and possibility of a caucus of non-judge members rendered the law defective. At the same time, the argument that the presence of the law minister or two eminent persons in the NJAC vitiated the system is hopelessly flawed. There is no jurisprudential principle or premise to assume that the inclusion of the law minister or eminent persons will taint the process of selection and appointment.

A POSSIBLE ANSWER

So, let me suggest some principles that could be incorporated in our Constitution:

1. The collegium shall have exclusive authority to *nominate* persons for consideration for appointment as judges of the High Courts and the Supreme Court.
2. A Judicial Appointments Commission shall review the candidates nominated by the collegium and *recommend* persons considered suitable for appointment to the President. The Commission shall be

broad-based (like the 15-member body in the United Kingdom) and shall have judges, jurists, legal scholars and the law minister.

3. A person nominated by the collegium and recommended by the Commission, and no other person, shall be *appointed* as a judge.

I am sure holes can be picked in the above principles. Just remember, in a democracy, there is no such thing as a perfect electorate, a perfect legislature, a perfect executive or a perfect judiciary. In their imperfections, they interact and make political, economic and social progress possible.

With a few deft strokes of the pen, the NJAC Act that was struck down can be changed to make it acceptable to Parliament, the Executive and the judiciary.

FOREIGN AFFAIRS

PARADISE LOST, WILL IT BE REGAINED?

25 October 2015

There cannot be a better moment for our closest neighbour Sri Lanka where all the planets seem to be smiling in the right houses. Before 1947, the phrase 'neighbouring country' stood for Sri Lanka and, some distance away, Burma. Pakistan and Bangladesh are latter-day neighbours. We had little contact with Bhutan until Jawaharlal Nehru made his famous visit riding on ponies for several days. Nepal was a reclusive kingdom.

SPECIAL BOND WITH SRI LANKA

There was always a special bond with Sri Lanka. The people of Tamil Nadu had close family and trade links with the Tamil-speaking people of Sri Lanka. There was a flourishing trade, and merchants, both Hindus and Muslims, set up shops near the port in Colombo. The streets still bear signs of their presence.

The north and north-east of Sri Lanka is the home of the Tamils. There are also many thousand Tamils working in the tea plantations. The educated, cultured Jaffna Tamil was a pillar of Sri Lankan society, especially in Colombo.

The land was occupied by the Portuguese, the Dutch and the British in that order. The British called it Serendip or paradise. Compared to the earlier colonisers, the British were benevolent to a degree and introduced the railway, the post office, the permanent civil service and the judicial system.

Sri Lanka became independent in 1948. The first Prime Minister, D.S. Senanayake, was a wise and far-sighted leader. It is said that he did not once leave Sri Lanka to visit a foreign country during his tenure as Prime Minister! He was succeeded by his son Dudley Senanayake. Both strived to build a plural society where all citizens were equal. All religions were equally respected. Sinhala, Tamil and English were the three official languages and all official business and commerce—including signboards and nameboards—were in the three languages.

THIRTY YEARS LOST

Short-sighted politicians brought ruin. It started with the 'Sinhala only' policy. Once the fire of divisiveness was lit, it was fanned by several elements. That fire singed Sri Lanka for nearly 30 years.

There is no need to go into history, especially recent history. The end of the internal conflict was brutal and bloody. There were gross violations of human rights as well the canons of international law. Much of these have been identified, but much more remains to be done.

Mr Mahinda Rajapaksa thought that he would be remembered forever as the President who defeated the Liberation Tigers of Tamil Eelam (LTTE)—and would be re-elected. He was wrong.

In quick succession, the people elected moderate Tamil leaders as chief ministers in the provinces of Jaffna and Trincomalee; an unassuming, low-profile former minister under Mr Rajapaksa as the new president; and an experienced politician as prime minister. Mr Maithripala Sirisena, the new president, is widely respected for his humility and integrity. Mr Ranil Wickremesinghe has been prime minister twice before and is regarded as resourceful and capable. What is unusual is that the President and the Prime Minister are the leaders of the two parties—Sri Lanka Freedom Party (SLFP) and United National Party (UNP)—that contested the last elections as worthy opponents of each other!

THE PLANETS ARE SMILING

None could have predicted that the following three momentous events would happen in Sri Lanka in the year 2015:

1. That the SLFP and the UNP would form a grand coalition government, notwithstanding the efforts of a section of the SLFP to undermine the arrangement;
2. That the conflict would finally end, the embers of the fire would finally die down, and the Tamils who had suffered the most would look forward to living in a united Sri Lanka as equal citizens; and
3. That the Tamil-speaking people would have moderate leaders as the heads of the two totally legitimate provincial governments.

What should India do as Sri Lanka's closest neighbour? Thankfully, the NDA government has continued the projects promised and started by the UPA government, including the ambitious 50,000 houses programme. It is commendable that the government has kept in place the same team in the High Commission and the Consulate. There is enormous appreciation of India's support to the nuanced resolution adopted at the last meeting of the United Nations Human Rights Council (UNHRC). India should press on.

- The housing programme is the flagship of India. India should offer to build more houses for the displaced and affected people as well as for the plantation workers who have suffered for decades.
- India should offer projects to both the northern and the eastern provincial governments and encourage them to work towards common objectives.
- India should offer technical help—if help is sought—in drafting the new Constitution that is a promise of the new government.
- India should use its moral authority to press for the implementation of the India–Sri Lanka Agreement and especially the devolution of powers to the provincial governments.
- India should allow the Sri Lankan Parliament and government to find a way to implement the UNHRC resolution.

- Above all, India must remain in close contact with Sri Lanka. The only minister who has visited Sri Lanka since May 2014 is the Prime Minister! The UPA government was equally remiss. The Prime Minister should despatch one minister every month to Sri Lanka with strict instructions to travel, listen and report (and not to say anything out of turn or tune).

HOW TO LOSE A FRIEND AND ALIENATE PEOPLE

6 December 2015

The government has come a long way since 26 May 2014. At least three neighbouring countries that stood and applauded the new Prime Minister as he was sworn in have distanced themselves from India. Others have become more watchful. In no case is this more evident than in India's relationship with Nepal.

Nepal has a special relationship with India. The two countries share a religious and cultural history. There is an open border. Nepali nationals fought alongside Indian soldiers in many wars and do so even today. The Gorkha regiment is known for its valour. There are an estimated six million Nepali nationals who live and work in India.

Since Nepal is a landlocked country, with India on three of the four sides, its outreach to the rest of the world is through India. The bulk of Nepal's trade is with India. Most of its supplies come from India or through India.

India has been a good and benevolent neighbour. It has extended special trade concessions to Nepal. It has extended aid. It has encouraged Indians to visit Nepal. There are many families in the two countries who are tied by marriage.

The Nepali Congress party was seen as a sister organization of the

Indian National Congress with shared political values. The Communist Party of Nepal had close ties with the Communist Party of India and, later, with both the Communist Party of India (Marxist) and the Communist Party of India.

THE BIRTH PANGS

Since the monarchy in Nepal was replaced by a democratic structure, Nepal has gone through a very difficult period of transition. There have been many short-lived governments and many prime ministers. The Constituent Assembly struggled for many years to draft a Constitution. India extended strong support to Nepal in its endeavour to become a Constitutional Republic. During this period of instability and uncertainty, India did not waver in its support. Trade and commerce continued as before. Open borders remained open.

All this was reflected in the outpouring of joy when Nepal received Prime Minister Modi on his first official visit to Nepal. Mr Modi made a fine speech to Nepal's Parliament. India–Nepal relations seemed to have touched a new high point.

How did that 'high' collapse to a point when all observers are agreed that Nepal–India relations seem to have reached the nadir?

TAKEAWAY FROM CONVERSATIONS

A few days ago I had occasion to meet some prominent businesspersons from Nepal. On a flight from Bengaluru to Delhi, Mr Kamal Thapa, Nepal's Deputy Prime Minister and Foreign Minister, was seated next to me. The takeaway from my conversations (without attributing any particular statement to any particular individual) can be summarised as follows:

1. There are issues concerning the Madhesis, but India should allow Nepal the space and time to resolve those issues through negotiations. While espousing the cause of the Madhesis, India should not pit the Madhesis against the rest of the population.

2. A new Constitution has been adopted by Nepal's Parliament. If it requires amendments, they can be made in due course after negotiations (just as the Indian Constitution has been amended over a hundred times).

3. There are about 112 constituencies where the Madhesis are dominant or have a significant presence. Only 11 MPs among them are opposed to the new Constitution.

4. There is one province that is comprised exclusively of Madhesi-dominated districts. They want another province with exclusively Madhesi-dominated districts. This is a matter that can be resolved through negotiation. It cannot be a cause for a blockade.

5. India intervened very late—beyond even the proverbial eleventh hour—to stop the adoption of the Constitution. When the Constitution was adopted nevertheless, India felt slighted, unjustifiably.

6. The people of Nepal—or certainly an overwhelming majority—believe that India has imposed the blockade and the Indian government has instructed suppliers, including Indian Oil, to stop supplies. Whatever may be the reality, that is the *perception*, and with the passage of time that perception is getting stronger.

7. Nationalist feelings in Nepal are riding very high, and the overwhelming majority of the people has turned against India. Even MPs elected from the Madhesi-dominated constituencies blame India for the blockade. That is why, despite three months of immense hardship and suffering, there is no protest by the people against the Government of Nepal. They are determined to face the situation bravely.

8. With a seasoned politician as External Affairs Minister, a highly skilled and experienced diplomat as Foreign Secretary and an astute security expert as National Security Adviser, how did India commit grave tactical mistakes in dealing with Nepal?

9. India made the mistake of attempting belatedly to block the adoption of the Constitution. India made the mistake of opposing (silently) the election of Mr K.P. Sharma Oli as prime minister. India made the mistake of propping up Mr Sushil Koirala as a candidate for prime minister when Mr Oli was all set to offer Mr Koirala the presidency.

10, Nepal expects Indian political parties and Parliament to assert themselves and direct a course correction before matters reach a point beyond repair.

BEING A GOOD NEIGHBOUR

Parliament is in session. The Congress and the Communist parties that have an international outlook have a special responsibility to initiate a debate on India–Nepal relations. A message must go that India is a good neighbour and a reliable friend who will abide by the rules of engagement between neighbouring countries.

SPUTTER, STOP. THEN, SUDDENLY, START

13 December 2015

Pakistan is there. It is on India's western border (and until 1971 was also on the eastern border). It cannot be wished away; nor can India pretend it will go away.

On the very day the two countries became independent, they inherited a clutch of problems that was the inevitable result of Partition. I know of no example in history where two countries born out of a division of land lived in peace ever after.

LEARN AND FORGET

History also teaches us that such countries must learn to live with each other, and the only way to peaceful co-existence is to talk to each other. If that means talking to each other every day or every week or every month, so be it.

That lesson was learnt and forgotten and re-learnt many times since 1947. Every government in India—and needless to say every government in Pakistan—was guilty on that count.

The period after the Mumbai terror attacks in 2008 was a particularly difficult period. It was akin to the post-war situation in 1965, 1971 and 1999. In a sense it was worse because it brought the conflict from the borders to the heart of India. The mood in India was bitter and implacably opposed to Pakistan: no to talks, no to exchanges, no to cricket, no to everything. The government could not ignore the anger among the people; yet there was no way forward but to negotiate the hurdles and find a way to engage with Pakistan.

The UPA governments (first and second) tried to do that, and got mixed results.

Fast forward to 2013. Enter Mr Narendra Modi. He had adroitly positioned himself as the alternative to Mr L.K. Advani, who was increasingly seen as not a winner. He had also successfully positioned himself as the alternative to the Congress party. Within the BJP, it was Mr Modi versus Mr Advani. In the country as a whole, it was Mr Modi versus the Congress.

Such positioning required a new rhetoric, laced with hyperbole, that presumably reflected the mood of the people. It is here that Mr Modi scored over every other political leader in the country.

MODI ON TALKS WITH PAKISTAN

In the context of Pakistan, let me recall some of the statements that he made in 2012 and in the run-up to the election in May 2014.

On 12 December 2012, Mr Modi said, 'Delhi is working behind the scenes, keeping people in the dark and making a deal with Pakistan.'

At Tiruchirappalli, Tamil Nadu, on 26 September 2013, Mr Modi said, 'Pakistan army can behead Indian soldiers. Still, the Delhi government eats chicken biryani with the Pakistan Prime Minister in the name of protocol.'

When the election results were a few days away, on 8 May 2014, a supremely confident Mr Modi, answering a specific question on the Composite Dialogue process, said, 'Is it possible to have a discussion amidst bomb blasts and gun shots? So, to have a reasonable discussion, first the blasts and the gun shots have to stop.'

The statements evoked both praise and concern. They appealed to certain sections that the BJP was trying hard to woo. They also raised serious concerns among diplomats and security experts. Was Mr Modi setting the bar at an impossibly high level that no talks with Pakistan would be possible during his entire term?

However, Mr Modi surprised everyone by inviting all SAARC (South Asian Association for Regional Cooperation) leaders, including the Prime Minister of Pakistan, to his swearing-in. It was a political masterstroke and led the world to believe that the rhetoric of the elections would be left behind.

IS THERE A STRATEGY?

In retrospect, every assessment was wrong. Neither the rhetoric nor the masterstroke was the result of a carefully thought out strategy. Much of it was impulsive. The months that followed proved that the new government simply lacked a strategy to deal with Pakistan. Recall the starts and stops and the twists and turns of the last 18 months. Invitations and cancellations and handshakes and cold stares left the world bewildered, as they did most discerning observers in India. The sum and substance of the last 18 months was that the Government of India had no policy on Pakistan.

It was also clear that policy-making had been taken away from the Ministry of External Affairs and vested completely in the Prime Minister's office. The Minister had been reduced to Minister for rescuing stranded people. Seasoned diplomats had been assigned crucial jobs in Event Management.

In the last few days, the government has sprung another surprise. Despite a 25 per cent increase in infiltrations this year over last year, reported by the Border Security Force, India and Pakistan have decided to talk to each other. Secret talks are no longer taboo. Back channels are no longer suspect.

Ms Sushma Swaraj has taken the position of centre-forward. Almost miraculously, the once-shunned Composite Dialogue has metamorphosed into Comprehensive Bilateral Dialogue. Everything is on the table—from Jammu & Kashmir to counter-terrorism, from Siachen to Sir Creek, from economic cooperation to people-to-people exchanges.

If all these are part of a serious strategy, we must welcome the change. There will be challenges and the ride will be bumpy but there is no substitute to staying the course. No one expects miraculous solutions to all the issues, but no one wants conflict or war.

GLOSSARY

Aadhaar	Unique Identity Number
AAP	Aam Aadmi Party
Abki baar, Modi sarkar	This time Modi government
Achche din	Good days
Achche din aanewale hain	Good days are coming
AFSPA	Armed Forces (Special Powers) Act, 1958
AJL	Associated Journals Ltd
Bhumi puja	Ground breaking ceremony for construction
BJP	Bharatiya Janata Party
Brent	Brent crude oil (price)
BSF	Border Security Force
CBI	Central Bureau of Investigation
CCTNS	Crime and Criminal Tracking Network and System
Chalo chalein Modi ke saath	Come, let's go with Modi
COPPY	Corresponding Period of Previous Year
CPI	Consumer Price Index
CPI(M)	Communist Party of India (Marxist)
CPV division	Consular, Passport and Visa division
Crore	10 million
CRPF	Central Reserve Police Force
CSS	Centrally-sponsored scheme
DBT	Direct Benefit Transfer
EAM	External Affairs Minister (Foreign Minister)
FA(DS)	Financial Adviser (Defence Services)

FFC	Fourteenth Finance Commission
FSLRC	Financial Sector Legislative Reforms Commission
FY	Financial Year
GDP	Gross Domestic Product
Ghar wapsi	Reconversion (to religion of forefathers)
GIFT	Gujarat International Financial Tec-city
Gita	A venerated Hindu holy text
GST	Goods and Services Tax
GUJCOCA	Gujarat Control of Organized Crime Act
GVA	Gross Value Addition
Hindu Hriday Samrat	Emperor of Hindu Hearts
IB	Intelligence Bureau
IIM	Indian Institute of Management
IIT	Indian Institute of Technology
IMD	India Meteorological Department
IMF	International Monetary Fund
IPR	Intellectual Property Regime
ISIS	Islamic State of Iraq and Syria
Jan Dhan Yojana	Financial inclusion programme
Jan Lokpal	Ombudsman
JD(U)	Janata Dal (United)
Jhoola	A traditional swing
Khap panchayat	An assembly of leaders of a clan
Kuchcha (dwelling)	Temporary, usually thatched, house
Lakh	100,000
LARR Act	Right to Fair Compensation and Transparency in Land Acquisition, Rehabilitation and Resettlement Act, 2013
Lok Sabha	House of the People (lower House of Parliament)
LPG	Liquid Petroleum Gas (for cooking)
MEA	Ministry of External Affairs
MGNREGA	Mahatma Gandhi National Rural

	Employment Guarantee Act
MLA	Member of the Legislative Assembly
MP	Member of Parliament
MPC	Monetary Policy Committee
NATGRID	National Intelligence Grid
Naxalite	Left wing extremist belonging to the Maoist party
NDA	National Democratic Alliance
NGO	Non-Governmental Organization
NHM	National Health Mission
Nirmal Bharat Abhiyan	Clean India campaign
NITI Aayog	National Institution for Transforming India Commission (that replaced the Planning Commission)
NJAC	National Judicial Appointments Commission
OROP	One Rank One Pension
Panchayat	Local self-government body in a village
PDMA	Public Debt Management Agency
PMI	Purchasing Managers Index
POL	Petroleum, Oil and Lubricants
PPP	Pubic Private Partnership
Prachar Mantri	Propaganda Minister
Pradhan Mantri	Prime Minister
Pradhan Mantri Jeevan Jyoti Bima Yojana	Prime Minister's Light of Life Insurance Scheme
Pradhan Mantri Suraksha Bima Yojana	Prime Minister's Security Insurance Scheme
PSE	Public Sector Enterprise
Rajya Sabha	Council of States (upper House of Parliament)
RBI	Reserve Bank of India
REER	Real Effective Exchange Rate
RJD	Rashtriya Janata Dal

RKVY	Rashtriya Krishi Vikas Yojana (National Agricultural Development Plan)
Rs	Rupees
RSS	Rashtriya Swayamsevak Sangh
RTI	Right to Information
Sangh Parivar	Sister organizations of the RSS
Sarkar, sarkari	Government, governmental
SC	Scheduled Caste
SEBI	Securities and Exchange Board of India
SHG	Self-help group
SIS	Special Infrastructure Scheme
SLFP	Sri Lanka Freedom Party
ST	Scheduled Tribe
Swachh Bharat	Clean India
UK	United Kingdom
UNHRC	United Nations Human Rights Council
UNP	United National Party
UPA	United Progressive Alliance
US	United States of America
VAT	Value Added Tax
Vikas Purush	Man of development
WPI	Wholesale Price Index
WTI	Western Texas Intermediate (price of crude oil)
YI	Young Indian

www.ingramcontent.com/pod-product-compliance
Lightning Source LLC
Chambersburg PA
CBHW050237270326
41914CB00034BA/1963/J